PROPHETIC RELATIONSHIPS

Ken Cox

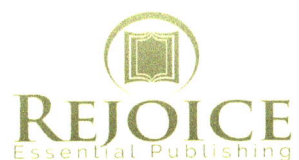

Copyright © 2025 by Ken Cox

All rights reserved. No part of this publication may be reproduced, distributed or transmitted in any form or by any means, including photocopying, recording, or other electronic or mechanical methods, without the prior written permission of the publisher, except in the case of brief quotations embodied in critical reviews and certain other noncommercial uses permitted by copyright law. For mission requests, write to the publisher, addressed " Attention: Permissions Coordinator," at the address below.

Ken Cox/Rejoice Essential Publishing
PO BOX 512
Effingham, SC 29541
www.republishing.org

Unless otherwise indicated, scripture is taken from the King James Version.

Prophetic Relationships/Ken Cox

ISBN-13: 979-8-3485-4212-2

TABLE OF CONTENTS

INTRODUCTION..1
CHAPTER 1: The Consequences Of A Prophet's Conflicted Soul...3
CHAPTER 2: The Problem With The Sons Of The Prophets........12
CHAPTER 3: The Importance Of A Prophet's Uncertain Walk....20
CHAPTER 4: The Prophet's Relationship With Poverty...............35
CHAPTER 5: Changing Emotions In A Prophet's Life (The Wisdom Of Conflict)...47
CHAPTER 6: Apostles / Prophets Understanding The Mentality Of Your Personal Destiny.......................................55
CHAPTER 7: Are You A Prophet God Trusts With Trouble, Or A Prophetic Peer Relationship?.............................62
CHAPTER 8: Mocking And Disrespect Of God's Prophets..........70
CHAPTER 9: Prophets Having Difficult Conversations With God...82
CHAPTER 10: Prophet In A Dry Land Or A Dry Season...............88
CHAPTER 11: Losing Your Normalcy As A Prophet.....................96
CHAPTER 12: Prophets Who Live By A More Sure Word...........103
CHAPTER 13: The Old Prophet Of Bethel And The Old Prophet Of Today..110
CHAPTER 14: Why Don't Today's Prophets Get Along Or Build Relationships?..121
CHAPTER 15: The Prophet's Attitude Of Responsibility.............127
ABOUT THE AUTHOR..133

INTRODUCTION

As the world evolves, it's intriguing to note that some things remain constant. Have you ever paused to assess the value of your relationships as a prophet? What about the value of prophetic relationships within your sphere of influence? These connections, often overlooked, hold a unique and profound significance in our lives and prophetic ministries.

Do you even have an opinion on your prophetic relationships? Let me assure you, my friend, you will, and you do have an opinion, whether you voice it or not. We all do because we are humans. Our shared humanity binds us through our feelings and opinions.

We all experience feelings in one way or another. While we may not express them similarly, the key is to understand and manage our feelings.

Allow me to introduce you to the world of Prophetic Relationships. This book is a reflection of prophetic interaction and observations. This book explores the prophetic world of today's gospel and leans on the lessons of our biblical prophetic gifts. While we will draw inspiration from the journey of our prophetic predecessors, this work is a testament to the transformative power of today's prophetic relationships.

Like many of you, I too seek genuine relationships with people who share the same desire. I am not ashamed to admit that I have faced my own struggles with prophetic relationships, as I have seen many others do also. One day you are their prophet and the next day you are forgotten. Then they are ordained, and the convenience of disappearing is now more important as you see them months, sometimes years later in another work.

I dedicate this book to those prophets who wanted to be friends and yet be themselves. They have seen that this is much easier said than done. The prophetic journey is a lonely and long walk, to say the least.

Real covenant relationships today among prophets are priceless. Know who they are and covet them. An acquaintance can come or go. They have the option to prove themselves as friends or confidants. The purpose of this book is to share some experiences and help us all in our relationships with God and each other as we grow and manifest into functional prophets of the now generation. Welcome, my friend, to Prophetic Relationships.

CHAPTER 1

CONSEQUENCES OF A PROPHET'S CONFLICTED SOUL

Since this book is about relationships among prophets, let's start with the person you see in your mirror. Let's talk about you, let's talk about me, and let us talk about us.

Have you considered the fact that you may be conflicted and that it's affecting your relationships? Few prophets we will read about in the Bible are more conflicted than David. David is the only person in scripture; the only one God said is a man after my heart.

We can also debate the authenticity of the prophetic calling in David's life. But what's more important is how his story can resonate with our struggles as prophets and how we can learn from his experiences.

As a prophetic teacher and author, let me state that I see David as a prophet. I'm sold out to the fact that David is a divine prophet. He is a different type of prophet, and yet, because of his extraordinary life and experiences, many fail to see him as a prophet of God and only focus on his time as king and his rise to that position.

David, the prophet, is a classic example of God being there, picking up one's life and doing what was needed, and now God seems to be absent. Let's now deal with our most personal prophetic relationship.

That would be us. What happens when your life is a mess, and you pray, you scream for God, and He is not there, and your situation seems to have gone viral?

Let's look at David's life as we look at our lives and the consequences of a Prophet's Soul, a conflicted soul of a prophet. In *2 Samuel 12:15-19*, we see that God moved on the prophetic word of Nathan.

The child of Uriah's wife with whom David has fathered a child, is now sick, and David pleaded with God. Notice that he fasts, goes in, and lies all night on the ground.

He is being watched as the elders of his house arise and go to him to raise him from the ground. We see that David did eat food with them. The child that David loves has now died on day number seven. Imagine if you were one of his servants afraid to tell him that his child was dead.

They speak among themselves, wondering how they will tell David. He did not talk to them, despite them being there to serve him. What he sees and hears are the whispers and mannerisms of his servants. David now figures out that his child is dead, as his servants and he finally speak, and they confirm that the child is dead.

David is dealing with what every prophet of relevance must deal with today. It is some personal scandal or personal chaos or drama. It is common knowledge that he has fathered a child with a woman who was married to another man, and yet that man was a man who loved him and was one of his troops. That's a known fact.

Another known fact is that man is now dead. Prophet, let's get real; people will know your business and may never say it to you, but talk oh so much behind your back. Welcome to David's world.

God has sent the Prophet Nathan to David. Nathan's role is crucial here as he has told David how God sees his situation and that God will deal with him through his child. The child dies despite David's prayer and fast. Pay attention to this fact.

In, *2 Samuel 12:20-23 20*, we see that David has arose from the ground. He has washed up and went to the house of the Lord and worshipped. Then he eats and speaks with his servants. He explains to them about the loss of his child. He mourns for the loss of his child and how the relationship with the child will be no longer.

Prophets, can you see that David is a strong man and he is now in total grief? The reality of the prophetic word of Nathan has set in. There is no doubt that David's anointed, but he has sinned, and his actions have cost him greatly. He has lost a child; it's common knowledge how he has lost the child. Here he is, the golden boy of his era, and his life is a mess.

This is no different than a scandal that we may endure today. Like David, we all run to God when we have made decisions that have cost us greatly. Here is a wonderful lesson we all can learn from David. David is known to repent when he is in trouble. The lesson is that prophets should never forget to repent when in trouble. Learn this from David.

David is in prayer repenting, and yet the burden of a child, an innocent child's life, is upon him, a child that will lose his life. To think that David is not thinking about this is an understatement as he petitions to God. Remember this: we are talking about David, who could be any of us.

Have you ever been in trouble with God, and everything you got came from God? He is in the middle of a scandal, yet he is teaching us another valuable lesson. The scandal in your life, prophet, is about how you respond to God. The scandal is not about how you respond to man. All now-generation prophets, need to learn this.

Prophet, when a scandal shows up in your life, and you want to know how to deal with it, understand that you must work your way back to God and not the opinions of men. Scandal today takes on the reflections of people and their opinions. While that may be the case, the reality is that scandal is about God and how you react to God and not men.

David has been put into a situation of great discomfort. He is now in the middle of a scandal, and it seems he can't escape it. How can David free himself from this when he is the cause of the situation? We all deal with this situation at some point in our lives.

Prophet, have you ever been in a situation where everybody knows your business? They are not talking to you, but they are talking about you. Some of it may be accurate, and some may be wildly inaccurate, but the constant in the equation is you.

You foul up, and you're conflicted because you need God to bring you out, and you see suffering because it appears God does not do what you need him to do.

Prophet, can you imagine this type of crisis in your life? A crisis will birth a conflict, and a conflict always has consequences. It is a type of crisis in which you can't blame the devil, your boss, this pastor or that pastor.

You can't blame this prophet or that prophet; it is the reality of knowing that you can only blame yourself and see that you're responsible for the issue in your life. This concept is not popular as you seek God for your relief, but there appears to be none.

You messed it up, like David, and you know it, and now you have become a prophet with a soul conflict. You are ambivalent, and you must seek God even amid your conflict, amid the drama of your loss.

David teaches us that even in the worst times, we are strengthened as we seek God with a spirit of humility, knowing that we are willing to take responsibility for what we need and stop blaming others. This is priceless.

David was tormented at the thought of his son dying, and he needed God to fix his situation, and he was willing to own it. How many prophets today are eager to own their situation in the presence of God?

Here is what you must see and understand: the fact that the child was dying was second to the fact that it was David's fault that the child was dying. This is the source of his torment; he knows it and must repent and deal with it.

Prophet, have you ever had to deal with a tormented soul, and you know why? You may not have told anyone, but deep down, you know why. How do you see your relationship with you going?

In context, we now see David being monitored because people want to know how he will react. Have you ever had everybody standing around looking at you in your drama, and they aren't talking to you but want to see what you're going to do?

They whisper among themselves that their child is dead and how David is going to react to finding out. David's discernment knew as he shouted at his servants that his child was dead. His servants confirmed it.

2 Samuel 12:20-23 says, David arose from the ground, washed and anointed himself. David knew he could do nothing but accept that he had done all he could do, and he had to move forth.

There may be tears in his eyes and pain in his heart, but God has spoken concerning the child's life, and David accepts it. Today, too many of us fail to learn this hard lesson.

We want to blame someone for why God allowed this to happen to us. We must blame someone. David blames no one. He prepares to honor his child and knows and understands why God has done things in the manner that he has. How many of us prophets are here with our walk with God? David finds the strength to move forth.

The inability of today's prophet to accept our issues, our failure to take responsibility, and our inability to discipline ourselves have played a significant role in our tormented souls and the problems that have been created. How much time have we wasted in our lives because we failed to deal with our issues?

Moreover, the fact that we have people who may suffer from our inability to accept the issues we cause is a measuring stick of our leadership mantle. We, the prophets and seers of this new generation, desire greatly to have no conflict; we want no issues, which is so unrealistic.

How many things have you blown off, ignored, or even abandoned and blamed anyone from the devil to your mama for the situation? You saw people suffer generationally, and you never did anything because the issue was not yours, but it was. You just passed it off.

When we examine ourselves, we must thank God for the example he shows us with David. Here is a servant of God who is conflicted within himself. How many prophets today are conflicted within themself?

You know you're a good person, but a part of you has caused you some drama because you made a decision that you knew may not have been in your best interest. How can David be so anointed yet make such an error in judgment?

Those of you who will be honest with me, will you ask yourself the same question? Prophets, what you will find out is that there is some good in the worst of us, and there is some bad in the best of us.

David's life teaches us to see ourselves as good and bad living together. If we learn nothing else from David, we must learn that. Can you exist and function knowing this?

Can you imagine the psalmist of Israel, the prophet of God, the chosen leader of God, the heir to the throne, and now he has orchestrated a murder, committed adultery, and has caused the innocent death of a small child?

How would you look at this person? The reality is that in some people's eyes, this will always be a source of gossip or personal feelings that many are unwilling to let go of their feelings.

This is especially true of gossiping prophets who will hide their issues and highlight their prophetic brother or sister. Keep in mind I have not even mentioned those outside of the prophetic Spectrum.

David realizes he has made a mistake, and the prophetic word he received from Nathan has now opened him up to the reality of his situation. This is what the true prophetic word will do.

Studying how David reacted to the word would have been so awesome to see how he handled the issue, to be there in person and see the interaction of two senior prophets.

Nathan brings the message, and David receives the message. What's obvious is that David had great respect for Nathan's mantle.

This is missing today in the prophetic. How many prophets deal with various facial features of disrespect when they say anything but a blessing? Most of us have lost count of the fact.

David teaches us another thing: receiving and healing amid our conflicted, stressful situations. Prophets, please understand that if you measure yourself out of your conflict by what people say, you're foolish because you're putting your status in the hands of man and not God.

Today's prophets are excellent at telling other prophets what's wrong with them, yet we don't feel we need to deal with ourselves like David. Lets explore even more the problem with the sons of the prophets.

Keep in mind when I say sons, I do mean both sons and daughters. Prophets learn the lessons of David; as we move into chapter two, the lessons are precious.

CHAPTER 2

THE PROBLEM WITH THE SONS OF THE PROPHETS

Let me start by defining the term for Prophet in Hebrew as Nabi (the plural is nebhiim or nebiim). Nebhiim has a root word of Nabu, which means to proclaim. We can also use the word to name or speak, which we do as prophets.

With their unique characteristics, prophets stand apart from the rest of society. Scripture provides evidence that prophets were part of a school or company. Today, we draw from this concept when we speak of the School of the Prophet.

Samuel was the head of a group of prophets; today, we would consider him an Apostle. Consider this in your culture (I Sam. 19:20). We see the great Elijah, who had a prophetic student in Elisha.

Submission and growth are the process; if we honor it today, there is no telling what we will see and experience. So often today, we extend such a half-hearted effort based on not getting mad, upset, or jealous, to name a few of our immature issues—small wonder our relationships are not where they need to be in the prophetic to grow.

Isaiah had prophetic students *(Isa. 8:16)*, and Jeremiah had a personal scribe prophetic armor bearer. These are examples of various types of prophetic relationships.

Strong, dynamic, charismatic prophetic personalities drew prospective prophets to them, a process we still see today. Those who seek to learn the methods and techniques of the prophetic gift are akin to the sons/daughters of the prophetic we know today.

Looking at our various cultures, these individuals were called disciples or followers of the chief prophet. Remember, our multiple cultures say a lot about how we identify prophets and even more about our interpersonal relationships. *2 Kings 2:3* is another reference to a term that did not imply physical descent but rather the embodiment of the spirit of 'the father.''

What is so hard to understand is that God does have a reason for our personal development. Look at Samuel, who was trained and prepared to be established by the prophetic priest Eli.

All the eyes of Israel knew Samuel as a prophet of God. His relationship with Eli was the key to his life.

Samuel went on to establish various schools for the prophets. Prophets came and were trained as students of the prophetic. Generally, these prophets lived together and supported each other.

They learned from each other in an atmosphere of unity and camaraderie. Genuine prophetic relationships were formed, not 2–3-day meeting covenant friends.

What is interesting as we study Prophetic Relationships is the story of The Gathering of the Wild Gourds *(2 Kings 4:38-41)*. The Sons of

The Prophets got the ingredients from the field. The unnamed prophet was sent out to gather herbs and find what he thought would make a good stew. Most of the herbs were soft, succulent plants.

But what he found out in the field were poisonous herbs. Untrained in these matters, the young Prophet mistook the wild vine for an edible herb. Some describe it as a leaf-like squash that is bitter and poisonous.

Consumed in large quantities, it would mess up one's digestive system and could even cause death. In smaller amounts, you might not die, but you might think you were going to and might even want to.

The point is that everyone was eating together, and what affects one prophet will affect us all. The actions of one prophet will reflect on others, whether we know that prophet or not.

Please focus here and reflect on how many times you have heard of one of your prophetic constituents, what they did, and the effect it has had on you, whether negative or positive. As prophets, we are like any other specialized field within the human experience but also unique in the spirit realm.

Prophets within this world are multiple poisonous ideas and issues that seem harmless but are bitter and bring unhappiness to man. Our development of discernment will not only allow you to recognize this but also empower you to protect others from these bitter herbs. We need relationships trained at all levels within the prophetic spectrum.

This is how we will help and equip other prophets. The prophet plays a crucial role in challenging current practices. The prophet must emphasize character within and through their ranks.

We are not upholders of traditions; we are the mouthpieces of God. Prophets are best recognized as charismatic personalities, Men and Women, who are compelled by an experience to utter the Word of God despite opposition, challenge, mockery, and imprisonment. This role of challenging current practices is not about rebellion or disruption but about ensuring that the community's actions and beliefs align with God's will.

The prophet must believe in God to represent his divine will. God's intentions, purposes, and actions are all part of this. Our words, as prophets, have the power to transform; this responsibility makes our role so significant and impactful. Let this inspire and motivate you in your prophetic journey. Build genuine relationships and start with God first.

This chapter is entitled 'The Problems of the Problem with the Sons of the Prophets. As prophets, we can only respond to what God requires and suffer the consequences in the conviction that God would prove the utterance true.

This unwavering commitment to God's will, even in the face of potential personal harm or societal rejection, is a fundamental aspect of the prophetic calling.

Prophet, this commitment can be likened to a 'death sentence' in the truest sense of the word, as it requires the prophet to put their own desires and safety aside in service to God's will. The prophet is constantly faced with challenges. We must have courage and dedication in the face of such challenges.

Being able to function in the most daunting circumstances fuels our faith and commitment to triumph. This resilience and determination are key in our prophetic journey.

One of the signature prophetic relationships in scripture is between Elijah and Elisha. Imagine the day that came when Elijah was to be taken away. He said unto Elisha, What can I do for you, son before I leave? Elisha said he wanted a double portion of the mantle upon his prophetic father in the faith.

Let's also note that Elisha refused to leave Elijah despite the sons of the prophets constantly inquiring about his status as he traveled with Elijah.

This is what relationships are about in the prophetic. He could have listened to the questions of his peers, the sons of the prophets, but he did not. The sons of the prophets never spoke directly to Elijah; they constantly spoke to Elisha. Here is the lesson of value. Prophet, notice how he did not gossip about his leader.

The mantle falls on Elisha, and when the sons of the prophets see this, they are amazed. They all knew that day at Jericho that the spirit of Elijah doth rest on Elisha. The respect he got from his peers as they came and bowed themselves to the ground before him was humbling.

Honor is the seed of access, and to walk in that type of honor takes a high level of humility. Prophet, understand that your peers will watch and honor you; when they see you, they will follow through and achieve.

Ask yourself: Why did the sons of the prophets not want to be a part of what was going on in Elisha's life? Here are some lessons to ponder. Why did they not step up and want to walk with Elijah? Sure, we know that Elisha was the senior prophetic son, but no one wanted to walk with him. Consider the following.

Only some will want what you want; some will always want to see if you succeed. Notice that Elisha told them to be quiet. He did not want to hear the rhetoric. Can we say nosey and a lack of courage and character? Consider it!

Elijah was the Head Prophet, and none of the sons of the prophets had the relationship with him to speak directly to him. What about the subordinate-level prophets?

It's funny how all the attention was directed at Elisha about Elijah. It's weird how none of the sons of the prophets thought it important enough to pursue what Elisha was doing.

These were his brothers and sisters, who saw it was fit to inform him of Elijah, but it was not essential to seek the reality for themselves as Elisha did. The point is that you must be a prophet of your convictions if God ever uses you. Others may say many things, but Elisha followed his conviction and shut others out who were the sons of the prophets. The early Schools of the Prophet offered us a unique perspective.

We should all wish we could have been at Ramah, Bethel, Jericho, or Gilgal prophetic schools. These schools were instrumental in teaching the prophets, the religion, and the Culture of Israel. They were about equipping.

Our schools today must finish and restore the lost concept of Relationships within the prophetic. They must be able to duplicate and adjust to society and the Culture of the current generation of prophets.

Prophets, it works both ways. The Culture of Seers/Prophets is maintained over the long term by building trust and open communication among each other. Prophetic meetings are only the starting point, not the finish line.

The next meeting you attend allows your peers to get to know you. Give them opportunities to see you as a real person maturing into a prophet of God. This is best done through your work ethic and your ability to participate.

Often, prophets bond at meetings and later find out you bonded with someone who attended the meeting and may hold different values than you do. They get assignments and just quit for no reason or claim God told them to do this, which is the opposite of what they swore at the meeting.

This is only one example of many. This is significant, especially as you are still getting to know who you are, communicating with someone you just met who may have habits you may not understand or are unfamiliar with, and you may have been influenced.

Let's look at the hard reality that you may have gossiped with that person about leadership, another prophet, or something that happened that neither of you understood.

Now, something happens with or to one of you. The issue creates awkwardness between you both. This has caused prophets to lose focus and create excuses as to why they can't do this or that. This is why you must understand one simple fact. Prophet, it works both ways.

The Prophetic Culture thrives when you empower prophets to help one another, to re-create the prophetic biblical community experience, and to feel like they truly belong. This is our purpose for The School of the Prophet and other such meeting environments, which are not created to entertain nor designed to allow you to show out on your peers.

Look at the School of the Prophet, which has today become a school of technical expertise and professional learning at a high level. We are the prophets of God, and we owe God our best and each other our best. This is why when something happens to one prophet, no matter how indirect it may be, it reflects on each one of us. While this is a sobering reality, it is a true thought.

We strive to Involve prophets in building this type of Culture — a culture of empowerment. You are here for a reason. Empower your peers to build strong anointed relationships as you are empowered to do so also.

This is the best way to help create a sense of belonging and connection. The ability to be upfront with each other is priceless.

Prophets want to put their best foot forward and make great impressions, but know that it is not by faking or showing out to prove that they are anointed or because they want to be seen because they feel the need to let everyone know that they should be on the program and they're not. Let's be real clear: This is not a social gathering; it is a school, a place of learning.

Far too often, meaningless "meeting talk" or unnecessary incidents ruin what could be beneficial and precious relationships among prophets/seers.

Understand you are here to build and be empowered as you empower others. Prophets, it works both ways. Let's expand on this as we talk about the Prophet's uncertain walk as we discuss Prophetic Relationships.

CHAPTER 3

THE IMPORTANCE OF A PROPHET'S UNCERTAIN WALK

How many of us today live in an atmosphere of certainty in this day and time? We are taught the importance of a sure walk with Christ from a young age.

Yet, as prophets, we must recognize that uncertainty is not a hindrance but a necessary element of our relationship with God. It is in this uncertainty that we learn to trust and submit. So, I ask you, is your relationship with God certain or uncertain?

The prophet who walks in uncertainty is a prophet whom God can send into any situation; in that situation, you can function. Every prophet of God must understand that embracing uncertainty is not a sign of weakness.

Prophets, please understand that as we embrace uncertainty, we see it is really the source of empowerment. It certainly births trauma and suspense in our lives, but it also equips us with the strength to face any challenge, making us feel confident and capable.

Uncertainty shields us as prophets from the details of the dilemma or the situation. God's blessing opens us to a learning process, forcing us to submit our intellect to God.

Your soul, my soul, we all submit to God's will for God to move in our lives. The problem we all have is that we want to know, but in uncertainty, we learn, fostering an open-minded and receptive attitude.

We want to know how long, how much longer, and how much more. We strive for the details, yet God says to trust him. Our development as prophets is delayed or suspended in direct relation to our ability to walk in the presence of God and not have all the details.

But in this uncertainty, we find reassurance in God's plan, making us feel secure. Faith in the prophetic realm is not debatable in any form or fashion.

Our base text is Exodus Chapter 16. The children of Israel are led out of Egypt by a prophet, whom we know as Moses, who is ridiculed, talked about, and blamed for everything that does not go as smoothly as they felt it should go, and above that, he's an outsider among his people.

Let's look at these things that are certain in the life of Moses. Take advantage of this fact. I say again that these things are confident in his life, and the details of each are readily available. His walk with God is uncertain as he proves he will trust God.

Think about this: You are walking in the desert for months without knowing, going on the word of God, and being led by an outsider. They constantly ask how much longer, how much more, and the stress is a test of Moses's mantle.

In reality, God did not give them details; they had to learn how to walk by faith and not by sight. This is why the prophet must learn not the details of life but the details of faith.

They wanted certainty, and what they got was uncertainty. They have yet to learn how to process what Moses was walking in, as he is a student of uncertainty in his prophetic development. God designs the atmosphere to teach us as His prophets the essence of prophetic faith. Again, prophet, learn the details of faith.

Moses came to lead them because of their distress. They cried out, and they couldn't recognize whom God had sent. This same issue still haunts prophets today, as God sends you and me into places we have never been, and the fact that we are sent there is proof of the prophets' prophetic development.

Moses has been through a development process, not just stepping out and showing up. His 40 years in the desert have prepared him, yet he is being tested in his first leadership assignment. This process of development, which includes preparation and testing, is a model for our growth as prophets.

Question prophet? Are you strong enough to absorb the wrath of critics in your life? Can you deal with the wishy-washy people who say one thing and do another in your life? Have you allowed yourself the opportunity to submit to God and walk in a level of uncertainty?

Uncertainty is not a sign of weakness but a critical element in our journey as prophets. It forces us to trust God and acknowledge that we do not have all the answers. Our issue is our need for more respect for our prophetic craft. We must learn and experience becoming a functional prophet rather than seeking titles and imagined importance.

We grab a title and then imagine our level of importance. This serves as the certainty we feel we need. We see no need for uncertainty as the common disrespect of our prophetic craft has become our norm.

We are so much like the children of Israel, coming out and complaining. We must learn to respect our craft enough to learn and experience it and not allow it to drive us to places of imagined importance that we have not earned.

Moses is a leader and God's Prophet. He experiences constant uncertainty, which we must discover is in God's presence, not man's. As prophets and people, we tend to identify people by how they express their faith in God.

As prophets, we often measure one's faith by their outward expressions. We identify the loudest and most active as having the strongest faith. However, the actual test of our faith lies in how we respond to God in the uncertainty and issues of our lives. Do we trust him, or do we not trust him? This is the accurate measure of our faith as prophets.

Prophet, if you want to develop, you have no choice but to understand that your faith will be tested beyond your being named a prophet; it will be tested in the very pit of your drama or chaos. This is how God will introduce and expose you as his prophet.

What are the steps you ask? They vary from prophet to prophet, but you must pass the training tests. One such critical area is Misplaced Rage. This refers to the anger or frustration directed at the wrong person or entity. The children of Israel experienced misplaced rage against Moses.

God introduced him as His prophet, and he immediately dealt with misplaced rage. They have become free people from the bonds of slavery, and now they are mad at God because they are dealing with situations in the wilderness that they are not used to. They now blame the prophet, the leader.

They should have blamed God, but the reality is that they do not know God like that. They see Moses as the outsider who has led them into a world of uncertainty. They have misplaced rage in Moses, and he is following God's directives.

You are the prophet. You need to see the lesson of why you need to walk in uncertainty in the presence of God so God can be the decision-maker in your life and not people's wishes. Your uncertainty forces you to depend on God and not your wisdom.

Most prophets never pass this test or understand that misplaced rage is anger and fear in others. It is generally directed at a leader, namely you, the prophet. This rage is usually directed at you for being misunderstood, and today, in the body of Christ, how often do we see this being played out?

Moses experienced it, and many of you in the prophetic have also experienced it or are currently experiencing it. They argue with you or against you, but they are really mad at family, church, or ministry and sometimes what they feel you stand for.

Prophet, learn the lesson of Moses, and that is that not everyone can walk with you. Who do you talk to? Who do you lead, and how do you, as a prophet, respond to misplaced rage?

Your response to misplaced rage is a humbling test in a society that fosters recognition and likeability as the tests of the prophetic.

Being seen and recognized is the model of success today, especially in the prophetic. There is no understanding of how to walk with God in uncertainty because there is not a miracle level of faith in God. Again, understand that to walk in uncertainty in God is to surrender and submit to God.

When a prophet surrenders and submits to God, the prophet's soul aligns with God's purposes. Your soul is healthy. Your soul is subject to God's will, and your mind is subject to the God; your will is subject to God's will. The reality is that you are walking in the presence of God, and your uncertainty is subject to God's.

This is the blessing of a prophet walking in God's presence in uncertainty. You now position yourself to see what you have not seen and go where you have not been.

Can you see why so many prophets have problems? There is no room in the equation for a prophet's ego. We want to know and be in charge, and since we know we have a gift, we fail to process submission unto God because we honor our gift more than we honor God.

The gift brings up notoriety; because of that, we feel certain in our walk. The level of humility is a lost function, as our hunger for the cheers of man is more potent than seeking God.

Prophet, you must understand the benefit of a walk of uncertainty in the presence of God. The prayers of His prophets sometimes look different from the answers that he gives. Still, we must submit to God and know that what God gives us is what we need.

Our walk of uncertainty in God's presence is the key to accepting what he tells us as we look for answers to the issues of our lives and prepare to work with others in their lives. The key is that you and I are not answering our own questions. We are trusting God without having to maintain the fanfare of people's approval of us as prophets.

Isaiah 55:6 says, " See God while he is near, and the unrighteous are to forsake your thoughts. Prophet, understand that your thoughts can and will betray you.

Have you ever spoken to yourself about thinking you would be here at a certain point in your life? Have you ever wondered out loud that you thought this and you thought that, and it did not come to pass? Have you ever thought higher of yourself than you should? Have you considered your thoughts towards others because you are a prophet?

Yet we see that the word tells us to forsake your thought prophets. If you really want to be a prophet of relevance working for God, then forsake your thoughts of what you thought. You and I are to be uncertain about everything except what God tells us. This is the essence of a relationship with God.

Let me be clear here: God did not promise to pay you according to your thoughts. God will pay you according to his word. Can you see how our thoughts are not in line with what God is thinking about in a situation?

We can impress upon ourselves to walk in a certain way and do certain things, but if we want God in our lives to do what we have never done, then we need to accept the fact displayed in the word of God that we walk in uncertainty as we seek God's directives. Every prophet must learn this, or you will be a legend in your own eyes.

The walk of uncertainty is the key as it allows God to take us places we have never been. When we listen to God's answer, we position ourselves to go where we have never been. We experience what we have never experienced.

This is why walking in uncertainty before God is the way of prophetic development before God. You will listen to God or His servant he has placed in your life. The life of Moses demonstrates this fact. After 40 years in the wilderness, Moses does not know what to do or how to address the situation.

He asks questions like, "Whom do I say sent me?" He references his stuttering issue. Moses is open to God and God's plan for his life. Moses is able to do things that he never thought or felt he would be able to do because he walks in uncertainty before God. The prophet learned this very valuable lesson.

How many of us today are walking in an atmosphere of certainly in our lives? We are taught from a small child the importance of having a sure walk with Christ. Despite all the teachings, there is a specific place where we must submit ourselves as prophets to walk in uncertainty. This is what a sure walk with God is for a prophet.

The prophet who walks in uncertainty is a prophet whom God can send in any situation and in that situation, you can function. While uncertainly birth trauma and suspense in our lives. Uncertainty shields us as prophets from the details of the dilemma or the situation.

Why uncertainly is such a blessing from God is that forces us to submit our intellect to God. Your soul, my soul, we all submit to his will for God to move in our lives. The problem we all have is that we want to know.

We want to know how much, how long, how much longer, how much more. We strive for the details and yet God says to trust him.

The reason our development as prophets is delayed or suspended is in direct relation to our ability to walk in the presence of God and not have all the details. Faith in the prophetic realm is not debatable, in any form or fashion.

Our base text is Exodus Chapter 16. The children of Israel are led out of Egypt by a prophet, whom we know as Moses, who is ridiculed, talked about, and blamed for everything that does not go as smoothly as they felt it should go, and above that, he's an outsider among his own people.

Let's look at these things that are certain in the life of Moses. Do not miss this fact. I say again these things are certain in his life and the details of each are readily available. What is uncertain is his walk with God as he proves to God that he will trust God.

Can you imagine walking in the desert for months and not knowing, going on the word of God, and being led by an outsider? They are constantly asking how much longer, how much more and the stress is a test of the mantle of Moses. The reality is that God did not give them details. They had to learn how to walk by faith and not by sight. This is why the prophet must learn not the details of life, but the details of faith.

They want certainty and they are getting what they feel is uncertainty. They have not learned how to process what Moses is walking in as he, himself is a student of uncertainty in the process of his prophetic development. God designs the atmosphere to teach us His prophet's faith. Again prophet, learn the details of faith.

The fact is that Moses has come out of the cries of their distress to lead them. They cried out and they can't recognize whom God has sent. This same issue still haunts prophets today, as God sends you and me into places we have never been and the fact that we are sent there is the proof of the prophet's mantle development.

Moses has been through a process of development; he has not just stepped out and showed up. 40 years in the desert have prepared him and yet in his first leadership assignment, he is being tested.

Question prophet? Are you strong enough to absorb the wrath of critics in your life? Can you deal with the wishy-washy people who say one thing and do another in your life? Have you allowed yourself the opportunity to submit to God and walk in a level of uncertainty?

Uncertainty is critical. It is important because it will force you to trust God and realize that you do not have the answers. The overriding issue for us as prophets is that we do not seem to respect our craft as prophets enough to learn and experience the process of becoming a functional prophet.

We grab a title and then we put ourselves on an imagined level of importance. This serves to function as the certainty that we feel we need. We see no need for uncertainty as the common disrespect of our prophetic craft has become our norm.

We are so much like the children of Israel, coming out and complaining. We must learn how to respect our craft enough to learn it and experience it and not allow it to drive us to places of imagined importance, that we have not earned.

Moses has the job of being a leader as well as God's Prophet. He walks in a constant level of uncertainty and what we must discover is that it is in the presence of God and not man. We as prophets and people have an ingrained tendency to identify people by how they express their faith in God.

We like to establish the loudest and most active as having the strongest or greatest faith. The reality you will find as prophets is that we are positioned by God by how we respond to him in the uncertainty and issues of our lives. Do we trust him or do we not trust him?

Prophet, if you want to develop, you have no choice but to understand that your faith will be tested beyond you being named a prophet. It will be tested in the very pit of your drama or chaos. This is how God will introduce and expose you as his prophet.

What are the steps you ask? They vary from prophet to prophet but you must pass the tests of your training. One such critical area is Misplaced Rage. The children of Israel experienced misplaced rage against Moses.

God has introduced him as his prophet, and immediately he now is dealing with Misplaced rage. They have become free people from the bonds of slavery and now they are mad at God because they are dealing with situations in the wilderness that they are not used to. They now blame the prophet, the leader.

They should have blamed God, but the reality is that they do not know God like that. They see Moses and he is the outsider who has led them into a world of uncertainty. They have misplaced rage in Moses and he is following the directives of God.

You are the prophet. You need to see the lesson of why it is important for you to walk in uncertainty in the presence of God, so God can be the decision maker in your life and not the wishes of people. Your uncertainty forces you to depend on God and not your wisdom.

Most prophets never pass this test or understand that misplaced rage is anger, and fear in others, and it is generally directed at a leader, namely you the prophet.

This rage is normally directed at you for being misunderstood and today in the body of Christ how often do we see this being played out?

Moses experienced it and many of you in the prophetic have also, or are currently experiencing it. They are arguing with you or against you but they are really mad at family, church, or ministry and sometimes what they feel you stand for.

Prophet learn the lesson of Moses and that is that not everyone can walk with you. Who do you talk to? Who do you lead, and how do you as a prophet respond to misplaced rage?

Your response to misplaced rage is a humbling test in a society that fosters recognition and likeability to be the tests of the prophetic. Being seen and recognized is the model of success today, especially in the prophetic.

There is no understanding of how to walk with God in uncertainty, because there is not a miracle level of faith in God. Again understand that to walk in uncertainty in God is to surrender and submit to God.

When a prophet surrenders and submits to God, that means that the soul of the prophet aligns with the purposes of God. Your soul's healthy. The emotions are subject to the will of God, your mind is subject to the will of God and your will is subject to God 's will.

The reality is that you are walking in the presence of God, and your uncertainty is totally subject to God's will. This is the blessing of a Prophet walking in God's presence in uncertainty.

You now position yourself to see what you have not seen and go where you have not been. Can you see why so many prophets have problems?

There is no room in the equation for a prophet's ego. We want to know. We want to be in charge and since we know we have a gift, we fail to process submission as unto God because we honor our gift, more than we honor God.

The gift brings up notoriety and because of that very fact, we feel certain in our walk. The level of humility is a lost function as our hungry for the cheers of man is stronger than seeking God.

Prophet, you must understand the benefit of a walk of uncertainty in the presence of God. The prayers of His prophets do not always look like the answers that He gives. Still, we must submit to God and know that what God gives us is what we need.

Our walk of uncertainty in the presence of God is the key to accepting what He tells us as we look for answers to the issues of our lives as we prepare to work with others in their lives.

The key is that you and I are not answering our own questions. We are trusting God without having to maintain the fanfare of people's approval of us as prophets.

Isaiah 55:6 says, "Seek God while he is near and the unrighteous are to forsake your thoughts." Prophet, understand that your thoughts can and will betray you. Have you ever spoke to yourself that you thought you would be here at a certain point in your life?

Have you ever wondered out loud that you thought this and you thought that and it did not come to pass? Have you ever thought higher of yourself than you should? Have you considered your thoughts towards others because you are a prophet?

Yet we see that the word tells us to forsake your thought prophets. You really want to be a prophet of relevance working for God, then forsake your thoughts of what you thought. You and I are to walk into uncertainty about everything except what God tells us. This is the essence of a relationship with God.

God did not promise to pay you according to your thoughts, but according to his. Can you see how our thoughts are not in line with what God is thinking about in a situation?

We can impress upon ourselves to walk in a certain way and do certain things, but if we want God in our lives to do what we have never done, then we need to accept the fact displayed in the word of God, that we walk in uncertainty as we seek God's directives. Every prophet must learn this or you will be a legend in your own eyes.

The walk of uncertainty is the key as it allows God to take us places we have never been. When we listen to God's answer we now position ourselves to go where we have never been. We experience what we have never experienced.

This is why walking in uncertainty before God is the way of prophetic development before God. You will listen to God or His servant he has placed in your life. The life of Moses demonstrates this established fact. Moses, after 40 years in the wilderness, does not have a clue as to what to do or how to address the situation.

He asks questions like, whom do I say sent me? He references his stuttering issue. Moses is open to God and God's plan for his life. Moses is able to do things that he never thought or felt he would be able to do because he walks in uncertainty before God. Prophet, learn this very valuable lesson.

CHAPTER 4

THE RELATIONSHIP OF PROPHETS AND POVERTY

There is a real and strong relationship between prophets and poverty. The marriage of the spirit of poverty and prophets is alive and well. The devil uses the spirit of poverty to destroy men and women of God, and especially prophets! Let's define poverty as a spirit that produces nothing good.

Poverty leads prophets to exist without living. Life is meant to be lived to the fullest. In the third Epistle of John 3:2, the stated wish is that you may be in good health as your soul prospers, which means every part of your life and being prospers. The spirit of poverty attacks the soul of a prophet.

Look again at *2 Chronicles 20:20.* It echoes, "Hear and obey God, and he will establish." Then he says, "Believe in his prophets, and you shall prosper." Prosperity is a critical theme in the word of God, associated with obedience to God. Prophets, we can't continue to ignore this, and statements such as *Deuteronomy 15:4* tell us there should be no poor, as God will bless the land as a special possession.

Most of us grew up under the teaching that money is evil. Rather than the truth, which is that the love of money is evil? Money itself is just a measure of value.

The problem many prophets and lay people have is a poverty mindset. Let us discuss this. A poverty mindset is destructive because it puts us in the role of a helpless victim. It tempts us to be spectators to our destiny. We believe everything that happens to us is the result of outside forces. We have no control.

The Bible commands us to be diligent and wise and promises that those traits inevitably lead to a prosperous life. The opposite of diligence and wisdom is folly and the life of the sluggard.

The Book of Proverbs teaches us the principles of hard work, discipline, sowing, and reaping. Every prophet should read and become familiar with these principles.

When we, as prophets, choose to embrace the poverty mindset, we refuse to acknowledge God. "He, meaning God, is in control, and God will make my life better." We make poverty an exception to God's word. We're saying, "I know what God says, "but."

Think about this for a moment. Poverty is an indication of a curse. *Proverbs 26:2* tells us that a curse is "Like a flitting sparrow. This in reality is a flying swallow, and now a curse without cause shall not alight."

Therefore, a curse requires a cause to align with. I am saying that poverty is the cause of the curse alignment within the prophet's life. The ability to keep the prophet down, broke, busted and disgusted is a now generation reality.

As a prophet and a leader, your whole nation or household can be cursed because of your disobedience. Do you realize that? Think and consider the curse of not giving. This produces living in scarcity and continual harassment from the devourer through financial misfortune, losses, theft, money going to cover sickness, or other unnecessary burdens.

Proverbs 13:18 says, "Poverty and shame shall be to him that refuses instruction...." An unteachable prophet hears but does not receive and act on the information given. It's not that they cannot learn; it's that they refuse to be taught.

A teachable prophet is willing to change once they have been shown a better way. An unteachable prophet will resist change because change is painful. A teachable prophet knows, "You must give up the way things are to have things the way you want them to be."

Proverbs 24:4 says, "By knowledge shall your chambers be filled. They all will be filled with precious and pleasant riches." Prophet, get this fact. The fact is that knowledge is power over the cycle of poverty.

Knowledge is essential to achieve prosperity. *III John 2* tells us our souls (mind, will, emotions) must prosper before our hands prosper. Knowledge determines how you think, reason, and respond to teaching regarding prosperity.

Proverbs 23:7 says, "As a man thinks in his heart, so is he." The power of God for prosperity seldom rises above man's thinking. Prophet? Do you think that you can handle being in a relationship with prosperity or poverty? The reality is you and I are making the choice daily. I desire not to be in a relationship with poverty.

The mentality of poverty manifests in the following mannerisms:

1. It resists thoughts of wealth and abundance, sometimes totally blacking them out of thought.
2. Turns a deaf ear to biblical teachings concerning the accumulation and management of money. This is why we see the prophetic gift so scrutinized.
3. Makes excuses for lack, need, and want in their lives. We always seem to find room for excuses, especially when we do not have the discipline.
4. Rejects any idea that things can change without financial insufficiency. Do we trust God or not? Who is our Father in heaven?
5. Becomes angry at teaching that promises blessings for obedient giving. We are going to have to overcome through God the pain of our past or the hurt that has led us astray and caused us to not trust.

To prosper, you must first break the cycle of poverty thinking. Use these basic steps to renew your mind.

1. Recognize and destroy your poverty thoughts.
2. Replace poverty thoughts with thoughts of prosperity.

Prophets understand that wealth itself is not condemned. *Genesis 13:2* says that Abraham had great wealth. In *Job 42:10,* God once again blessed Job with material possessions. In Deuteronomy, Proverbs, and Ecclesiastes, wealth is seen as evidence of God's blessing (*Deut. 8; 28; Prov. 22:2; Eccles. 5:19*). Stop allowing people to convince you that wealth is ungodly.

But we are not to trust in wealth but trust in God. *Prov. 11:4,1 Timothy 6:17 and James 1:11; 5:2* teach that we should not trust in wealth but in God. The Prophet *Amos (4:11; 5:11)* spoke against the injustice of obtaining wealth through oppression or fraud.

The Prophet Micah spoke out against the unjust scales and light weights with which Israel defrauded the poor (6:1). Neither Amos nor Micah condemned wealth; they only denounced the unfair means by which it is sometimes achieved. The Bible does not condemn those who are wealthy. But it does warn us that if God blesses us with wealth, we must keep our priorities straight and guard against the seductive effects of wealth.

Matthew 13:22 says, "The deceitfulness of riches chokes the word of and takes power from the word, making us unfruitful or unproductive."

Many prophets experience failure to harvest. When you do not gather spoils, a poverty mentality is set against you. The enemy waits until your harvest time and steals your blessings. In Judges 6, the Midianites always stole the harvest.

When we, as prophets, fail to steward our spoils or resources, a spirit of poverty will begin to develop its war plan against us and our individual situations. We see prophets wanting to increase without developing the storehouse to contain spoils. The enemy will always gain "automatic access."

As prophets, we can talk about being anointed and appointed, but when we don't exercise the principles of God because we don't want to give or refuse to give, it only fuels the divisive plan of the enemy that exists within our ranks.

This serves to notice to our ranks the validation that we simply are not prepared to handle seeing prosperity in our lives. In this case, we are simply another prophet who fails to develop a prosperity mindset but takes comfort in a poverty mentality.

As prophets in the Body of Christ, many of us fear to wage war against the spirit of poverty. We seem content with seeing Satan be better to his people than God is to His, and while that is a lie, we silently support it by the way we handle our giving and prosperity in general. We don't understand it or its dynamics.

The war on poverty is the conflict necessary to conquer your enemies and take possession of what God has promised to you. War is the grace to fight *(I Thessalonians 5:8; II Timothy 2:3,4)*. War is the receiving of the necessary armor for victory *(Ephesians 6:11-17)*.

Without war, we don't get an opportunity to enter into victory *(Revelation 3:21)*. The Lord brought His people out of Egypt by armies (Exodus 12:51), with a trumpet sound and a battle cry. He brought them out with the Ark *(I Samuel 4:5,6)*.

He used forces of nature if necessary to help them defeat their enemies *(Joshua 10)*. He always releases strategies enabling us to plunder, prosper, and stand *(Matthew 10; Ephesians 6)*.

God has a banner of victory for every prophet who will choose to employ His battle plan. HE IS still THE LORD OF THE ARMIES *(Romans 9:29)!* He already has victory for you! How do we, as prophets combat poverty by being kind and generous to others?

We combat poverty by developing strategies to help those who have been ravaged by poverty. We, as prophets, should help others gain wisdom on how to break out of the system that Satan is using to hold them captive financially.

All prophets need to understand the three major deceptions regarding money and prosperity. All three deceptions are based on Satan's lies.

TRADITIONAL DECEPTION: This is deception based on thinking that has been handed down from previous generations and accepted without question. Many well-meaning teachers, as well as parents, are responsible for this deception.

Religion has associated poverty with godliness. To think you cannot prosper because a parent or loved one told you that no one in your family tree has ever prospered is a deadly deception.

DOCTRINAL DECEPTION: Most have been taught that poverty is supported by misrepresenting scripture taken out of context such as teaching that says, "Money is evil." The Bible does not say money is evil; it says the love of money is evil *(I Timothy 6:10)*. Another teaching says Jesus was poor, so we are to be poor. Jesus had a ministry team of over seventy people.

So today, we see a preacher who can't afford to bring in another, and Jesus had seventy. *II Corinthians 8:9* says, "For you know the grace of our Lord Jesus Christ, that though he was rich, yet for our sakes, he became poor, (this is talking about the cross) that you through his poverty might become rich."

EXPERIENTIAL DECEPTION: This is the deception that is produced by the experiences of life. When elephants are small, circus trainers will chain them with steel leg irons to keep them confined to a certain area.

As the elephant grows, the leg irons can be replaced with ropes and wooden stakes. Even though the large elephant could easily break chains as well as ropes, over a period of time, the elephant is convinced that escaping is impossible. This is the mentality in the Body of Christ over money.

The same thing is true with humanity. The experiences of life confine you. Each negative thought regarding success and prosperity is like a steel bar that is connected to other steel bars until they form a prison of poverty.

We can reverse the curse and cycle of poverty by uprooting deception and embracing the truth as it is taught in God's word. God wants you to prosper.

We must learn how to develop reaping strategies *(Amos 9:13)*. The problem is when prophets fail to communicate. This is an issue. We cancel each other's effectiveness because we fail to develop a Prophetic Economy, the level of being that is above our problems. In other words, the solutions to our financial issues through empowerment.

In *Deuteronomy 8:18,* God gives us all the ability to be a success to accomplish His plan for each of our lives. *Joshua 1:8* says, "This Book of the Law shall not depart from your mouth, but you shall meditate in it day and night, that you may observe to do according to all that is written in it. For then you will make your way prosperous, and then you will have good Success."

As a prophet, Joshua learned that success occurred as a result of his behaving wisely and acting prudently. For a prophet, success occurs when we study to develop skills and understanding.

Scripture physically describes wealth and prosperity measured in terms of land, houses, servants, slaves, and precious metals.

The prime example is King Solomon, whose great wealth is described in *1 Kings 10:14-29*. This wealth was a manifestation of what God had given him!

To understand the difference between wealth and riches, look at this. Prophets understand that riches is receiving the grace of the Holy Spirit to enable you to accomplish what you are called to perform.

Riches are linked with accumulation or what you have amassed. A stewardship plan is devised from your riches.

The more you steward your riches properly, the more you will get. Prophets we steward by using God's plan of giving and managing. God is looking for prophets who will shift in their stewardship, so He can release a transference of wealth.

Giving is more than sowing a seed. It is a covenant relationship of worship. For a prophet to give, it says that you recognize God and His laws, and you bless Him with your substance and He blesses His prophets outwardly, even in the presence of their enemies.

Giving is worship. The worship of giving occurs when you respond to authority with generosity and blessing. Giving occurs when you realize what is lacking is blessed and empowered by the greater. Real giving occurs when you do not hold back what you have been entrusted with by the Lord! That is the essence of worship.

Prophets, God has a plan! Now is the time! Break old cycles of poverty in your life. Breaking the spirit of poverty is going to take prophets and other leaders to boldly declare the promises of God regarding wealth.

The culture in many churches today softly conveys the idea that it is more spiritual to be poor than to be rich.

Leaders, especially prophets, cannot speak passionately about Kingdom issues and then slip into an apologetic tone when it becomes necessary to address "the unpleasant topic of money."

The topic of money is unpleasant because:

1. We do not understand it and how it works
2. We have been subjected to spirits within people who love money and its value more than God. Examples are the greedy spirit, the lust spirit, the dumb spirit, the I'm better than you spirit, and the cheating spirit, just to name a few.

As a result, we are not boldly led into the promises of God regarding wealth. God is not seen as the real source of all material needs, which dishonors Him and robs the Body of Christ of the finances that should underwrite the aggressive expansion of the Kingdom!

We, most prophets, really don't know that the Word of God works concerning finances because we never put it to the test. Faith that can't be tested is faith that can't be trusted.

We don't have faith for our money or our resources, but we have faith for other sources that address issues we consider sinful and distasteful and we have faith for other people's money as long as it does not tax or affect us. We simply take God out of the equation by our fear of stepping forth.

The spirit of poverty is actually a spirit of fear. The voice of the spirit of poverty that does not recognize God as the true source of our material needs. God gave you the need for food, clothing, housing, transportation, training, and celebration, as well as many other things.

The resources of heaven are waiting to be tapped for the rapid advancement of the Kingdom. It also pleases the Father (heart of God) to pour out His goodness.

As prophets, we need to teach those who we mentor prophetically and the world that we should give everything without withholding anything for whatever reason. God gives whatever results in life we get based on our obedience or disobedience.

When the Israelites disobeyed God, they paid the penalty by being caged in a wilderness for forty years. They received manna just to keep them alive while paying for their sin.

As prophets, this happens to us when we disobey His principles. God allows us to survive on manna that is just enough to get by and scarce enough to continue looking forward to being free from such mere survival.

The Lord disciplines those he loves, and he punishes everyone he accepts as a son *(Hebrews 12:6)*. God disciplines us when we disobey His biblical financial principles. His discipline is what enables us to return to His ways when we stray.

He allows a financial curse or wilderness to develop in our lives. To Him, disobedience to His biblical financial principles is robbery. We rob God of what belongs to Him. He said, "Will a man rob God? Yet you rob me…in tithes and offerings. You are under a curse – the whole nation of you because you are robbing me *(Malachi 8-9)*."

As prophets we are to "seek first His kingdom and His righteousness and all these things will be given to you as well *(Matthew 6:33)."* Doing this means the prophet is to receive and impalement His word on finances and prosperity. God has given His ways to open the floodgates of heaven.

There will always be prophets who may decide to look for their own ways they consider more convenient. All sorts of "justifiable" excuses may come up. The most common are, "I don't have enough to give anyone," "I've so many critical obligations that giving would not be practical," and "I've not yet started earning my own income."

Have you ever noticed how prophets always want to devise other ways to receive from God without giving anything? Long prayers are sometimes accompanied by fasting.

Some prophets, who clearly misunderstand spiritual warfare, resort to binding and rebuking demons from holding their material blessings. Then we have those prophets who believe that living day-to-day on subsistence provisions by the grace of God could be His will for our lives.

God still waits for us to apply what He has prescribed for us. Until we respond according to His word, He continues to wait. Resorting to sinful ways and other worldly ways only brings worse problems in the long run.

While we know that sometimes prophets do have other issues outside of giving that may be contributing to financial woes, there also are hindrances to what God has promised through His word. Let's discuss this as we look at the emotional relationship of the prophet and the essence of the call upon a prophet's life.

CHAPTER 5

CHANGING EMOTIONS IN A PROPHET'S LIFE (THE WISDOM OF CONFLICT)

There is a fact that some people will only like you when you are in a certain position. Consider this: maybe you know or you are that person always in need, and all of a sudden, there is a change in your life.

The person who was always your friend is not anymore. Let me explain. Think about this: You now come into some good fortune, and your life changes and the one who was your friend suddenly changes on you. How many of us have had to deal with this in a relationship?

Prophet, has anyone ever changed you to the point where they have done a total 360 and left you hanging, wondering why they are acting like that? I wonder if anyone has experienced that. I can honestly say I have.

They saw your struggle, and now you are not struggling. You now see your way clear to accomplish your goals, and your supposed friend is acting crazy. Do not be afraid to say "Amen."

Let's meet David. We can argue whether he is a prophet or not, but the reality of his life is an example to every prophet of how God works with us and teaches us in the arena of life.

Let's start in *Psalms 69:4*. David explains to the reader that his brothers hate him for no reason at all. He goes on to say he is a stranger among them. He is talking about his mother's children. I'm talking about relationships here and setting order. Look again at what he says. He says, "I have become an alien, an outsider," and some versions say he became a stranger to his mother's children.

Why? Because they have grown up and are at an age of understanding, and they know that David is different from who they are. You can't overlook this point. Look at the dynamics of this relationship and see the emotional storm in David's life.

Why is David saying this? Look at *Psalms 51:5,* where David says he was born in sin. He speaks here of being an outside child. He asks God to purge him with hyssop. Once this happens, he believes he will be clean. David asks God to wash him; he will be whiter than snow. Here he fully realizes the changes within his life.

David is an outside child; in biblical times, he would have been referred to as a bastard child. The implication of Jesse not being his real father was clearly felt when the prophet Samuel told Jesse to gather his sons, and one of them would be the next king. As the prophet looked upon the sons, none of them were the one. David was not there; he was with the sheep and livestock on the mountain in the field.

We speak now of David, but you're also an outsider. You're in the group, but the fact is you are not part of the group. You find yourself different, and no one in the group can relate to you.

Being different has cost you and subjected you to multiple negative emotions from your friends, family, and even sometimes your prophetic peers, including yourself.

You experience multiple emotions from others in your life, primarily negative towards you because you carry yourself as a prophet of God, and the conflict seems always to be stirred towards your direction.

Welcome to this tool of God and how it plays out within your life. Understand the way of God as He separates to develop the emotions within us based on what is happening to us. Can our emotions answer the question about what is happening to us?

Welcome to David's world and those of you who can relate. Conflict comes into play as we see Goliath come on the scene and threaten Israel. Day after day, he insults everyone and finally King Saul proclaims that he will reward anyone who can help deal with Goliath.

Jesse, David's stepfather, has David come to bring lunch to his brothers who are on the scene and all of a sudden, he starts to speak that Goliath must be dealt with.

Notice his older brother, Eliab, and his negative attitude towards David *(1 Samuel 17)*. David has stirred up the gathering of men who have assembled to watch themselves, their country, and their families be insulted by Goliath, as King Saul's inability to deal with Goliath is clear.

Prophet, look at this. The conflict birthed an opportunity for David to elevate himself as a leader and as the next king, as he had already been anointed by the prophet Samuel. The conflict has birthed this in

David's life. Consider what conflict has birthed in your life. Think about this for a moment.

All conflict in your life, prophet, is not bad. Without conflict, there would not have been such a unique opportunity for David. Consider the conflict in your life. Would you be where you are now without some conflict?

What does conflict do? Conflict makes you stretch and sharpen to confirm who you are. God will use conflict in the life of a prophet to elevate that prophet.

Those prophets who desire and know that God has called you to nations, listen closely; until you learn how to deal with conflict, God will not send you to the nations. You may go on your own, but God will not send you. Conflict ignites the process of faith and knowing how to persevere during a struggle. Let's be real. Every prophet of God will struggle. It is by the design of God.

Those of you who proclaim the prophetic, understand that if you have had no struggle, you will, and if you run from the issue of conflict, you will not be fit to carry the prophetic mantle.

Look at David's life again; he defeats Goliath and is now in line for the King's reward. There is another issue. Let's look at the facts. He is no longer in the field on the mountain. He is living in the palace.

He has been given charge of men, and we see in 1 Samuel 18 that he is doing well, and his men are also. Saul is happy until David returns from battle one day, and women sing that Saul has slain thousands, but David has slain ten thousand.

The scripture tells us Saul changed from that day forth as he now saw David differently. Emotionally, from that moment is different from David. Today, we refer to it as jealously.

Prophet, think right now and consider who now sees you differently. As long as you were lost, confused, and could not see or take care of yourself, your friend was there, but now God has raised you up, and you are ascending in the will of God; all of a sudden, your friend has done a 360.

Prophets, the question I put before you now is, can you handle role reversal in your life? Emotionally like Saul, has anyone changed in your life and you are still trying to piece together what happened?

You now have what they sought, and they don't know how to adjust to the fact that your elevation may be the key to the continuous conflict within their lives.

Consider this because every prophet is unique, which may be their steppingstone to elevation. The shame is that we normally do not see it that way.

Look at this again. Saul has changed; his feelings, thoughts, and perspective have changed because David has been elevated in the eyes of his peers. When people can't justify your elevation, they will try to destroy you.

Look at Saul. His jealousy has now become his validation of killing David. Take a minute and process the changing emotions around and within your life, the prophet.

The saga continues in David's life as he escapes Saul's anger and is forced to unite with the Philistines. Saul seems determined to hunt

David down and kill him. That is just as much a reality as those who try to destroy you by reputation, rumor, gossip, and sheer evil.

Can you understand the emotions here? One minute, he was a son, and now David is hunted like he is an animal that needs to be killed. The emotions and how they can change in your life prophet move precisely like that. We all have to deal with it in one form or another.

David's saga takes him to unite with the Philistines, but after about two years, they separate. David has 600 men who follow him and are loyal to him. They are following their established leader.

Imagine David and his men on the way home to Ziklag. War is still going on. They approach Ziklag, and it is in smoke.

They come home to Ziklag and find their wives and children, family and family heirlooms gone. Look at this scene as they witness Ziklag burned with fire, and all is lost. The impact of this vision brings a group of warriors, grown men weeping. The scripture says they wept until they were out of strength.

Six hundred men followed David, weeping and crying out as David was also weeping and crying out for his family. What is so ironic is that those same men are now planning to kill David.

The same David that they have followed into battle, the same David that they have believed in and now the same David who they blamed for the loss of their families, instead of taking responsibility for the decisions that they made as they left their families to follow David.

This is where a relationship with God is so critical, prophet. Their emotions changed quickly. Prophet, how many times have you seen this? People want to blame everyone but themselves for their situation.

They will not take any responsibility, none at all and are super quick to point a finger at you as a prophet for what they refuse to do. Examples of this are they refuse to pray, give, and even show up sometimes and did I say believe?

The prophet learns the lessons of emotions and the anointing of conflict. These are simply two things that God will use to prepare you for your elevation. Could you not run from conflict and deal with it?

Relationships within the prophetic realm are subject at best until you realize the following. So, take this, if you will, as advice. You are a prophet, and you need to remember these two very important facts.

Surround yourself with other gifted people. People who are as gifted as you are in your gift. The exposure will force you to grow, as you will see and experience their excellence, and it will expose and explode your ideas and perceptions. This is how you will grow and stay true to yourself. Get around gifted people in their fields and learn.

The second point here is that when you have a friend in the prophetic, you do not have to speak with them daily. Stop falling into the place where you can't make a move unless they know.

Real prophetic friends want to see you grow and mature. This works both ways. They know that God's plan for your life may have you in another city, town, or even state.

They are cheering for you and not to control you but to see you prosper and vice versa. The reason for this is that they need you to grow as much as they grow also. Learn how to cherish your friendships within the prophetic circles.

Prophet, my challenge to you today is to learn how to recognize and deal with the changing emotions of people in your life. Will it happen?

Yes! You're Job then will be to recognize it and grow with the conflict it may deposit within your life. Prophet, you will grow by employing the following in your emotional health.

Being honest and speaking love fosters trust and openness among those you encounter! Learn how to acknowledge emotions and bring your feelings to God in prayer and worship.

Encourage and support discernment; when the prophet learns how to navigate spiritual awareness, the prophet becomes proficient in balancing biblical truth vs. personal feelings.

Have you ever considered why you may not have a clue as to your personal destiny? Are your emotions keeping you in a holding pattern with God? Can you handle the unstable emotions of those around you?

When the prophet learns emotional stability, their gift will help create and establish opportunities for others to grow and deal with emotional struggles. Let's talk about this.

CHAPTER 6

APOSTLES / PROPHETS UNDERSTANDING THE MENTALITY OF YOUR PERSONAL DESTINY

Have you ever felt that you have been a barrier or a block to your destiny? According to *Ephesians 2:20,* the apostle and prophet are the foundation gifts of the church, with Jesus as the chief cornerstone. The foundation gifts of the church are often the most scrutinized and the most attacked. I feel we all can relate to this in one way or another.

How many groups of believers do we see who are intent on not including these two gifts of the 5-fold ministry within their church or fellowship? Some would instead block out the apostle and the prophet for various reasons. Have you ever wondered why people act the way they do towards prophets and apostles?

Consider the fact that some have been hurt, and some have not been educated in the 5-fold ministry concept of Ephesians chapter 4. The foundational gifts of the apostles and prophets were not considered relevant in the church and ministry they grew up in. Then there is the fact that some do not believe in a 5-fold ministry.

All that is true, and it continues to be an issue, but what about the apostle and prophet who need to understand but do not understand their process of destiny? Over and over, we see these apostles or prophets who are in love with tomorrow and not today. They are in love with who they want to be tomorrow and fail to address the issues of their lives today. Can you relate to this?

Today is important because without today, tomorrow does not matter. Reaching your destiny is learning how to master your current step on the way to your next step in life.

Are you, the prophet or apostle, searching for validation, a place to place within the body of Christ, and you never seem to find it or grow? They do not realize that in the struggle to understand and grow, they could be the biggest obstacle to fulfilling their God-given destiny.

What holds a prophet or apostle back from building fruitful and anointed relationships? What is the issue of life that has these anointed servants of God in a place of stalemate? The problem happens far too often, and we must look into the word of God to find an issue.

Turn your attention to *1 Corinthians 13:11*. When I was a child, the word of God says that I thought, talked, and acted like a child. When I became a man or woman, the word says that childish things were put away. This is so important because we look at the world in a certain way.

Look closely at *1 Corinthians 13:11*. There are two different communication systems. The two systems need to be addressed in the life and work of the apostle or prophet. There is the system of the child or immature mentality and the system of being a mature adult.

We need to examine each to understand its effect. This will influence the life of an apostle or prophet as far as development. This is directly affected by how we see our destiny. The destiny of an apostle or prophet will never be understood or reached until they change their communication from child to adult.

Thinking, speaking, and understanding as a child differ from thinking, speaking, and knowledge as an adult. Let's examine how we look at others and ourselves. We will always test others by how they think, speak, and what they do or do not understand.

As apostles and prophets, when we look at our ministry work, do we have the courage to test that we may operate as kids or children when our position requires us to operate as adults?

What are we communicating or holding on to that limits our assignments and clouds our destiny?

This is the key to understanding our destiny. Do we function at the level we need to, and more importantly, are we aware we need to test ourselves? This is a fair question; we need to ask ourselves!

How many of us know and understand that many of us with prophetic and apostolic gifts are loyal to our own dysfunctions? How many of us in the apostolic or prophetic are stubborn enough to hold on to ways that clearly are not working?

Prophet, we claim growth, but it is not leading you to your destiny because you may be thinking, acting, or even communicating as a child. How many of us have heard phrases like "That's how I am, or speak for yourself"? We have all heard, "This is how God told me to do it." We love to blame God for misplaced childish behavior.

Why do we not consider that the way we say we are is not working? A better question is, how long will so many of us hold on to our dysfunctions and allow life to pass by simply?

We are doing things as children in an environment that we need to do as adults, and we are hurting ourselves. Today, we see the differences between prophets and apostles even within their ranks. Our childish ways have separated us greatly within the ranks of the apostolic and prophetic. The core issue that separates them is how and what they communicate.

This is how they speak, how they think, and how they act. Can you see that the way you think, speak, act is your announcement of your maturity or you being immature or childish? This is the link to your destiny. It is hard to understand that God is putting you in positions of influence and because of how you see them and how you feel about them, you are not understanding your journey to your destiny.

This is so critical to the prophet and apostle as they relate to the Body of Christ. The real issue is the inability to understand the need for change in an apostle or prophet. This is the status of the inner man.

What am I saying? The outer life of the apostle and the prophet are seen, and they are fine. Our outer life matures, but the real issue is that we are children internally, and we demonstrate it with immaturity.

David was king and still acting like a child on the inside? He was acting like a child, and what he wanted, he knew was not his. We all know about his situation with Uriah's wife. He was mature, but his actions were childish and selfish.

David becomes a modern-day metaphor for us to demonstrate that we are, in many ways, still children. We are grown on the outside but a kid on the inside. We look at our lives as children. Are we, as apostles and prophets, ignoring our childish ways? Are we are still trying to lead others?

What is the answer? Look again at 1 Corinthians 13:11 and see a keyword: "but." You can put away your childish ways, but that will not make you a man or a woman. Again, David was a full-grown man but still a child on the inside.

Throughout the Body of Christ, we have apostles and prophets who are fully grown and yet still demonstrate childish behavior. They are of age; they are in positions of authority, yet their influence is that of a child. They have not put away their childish ways. There is no understanding of what it means. This is a choice that they have not exercised because of a lack of understanding of the power of changing a mentality.

Can you understand that many of us in the apostolic and prophetic are still childish on the inside?

We have actually outgrown the way we communicate, think, and act. We have only done this on the outside, but not on the inside. This is where we need to make the changes.

How many of us will admit that we have outgrown the way we act? Sometimes, we speak one thing, and we actually mean something altogether different. Do we realize that we need to put some things away? What are we loyal to?

We are to put some things away in our lives, such as our childish actions. They are systematically killing us and destroying our relationships with each other. Our growth as foundation pieces of the gospel will never be realized until we understand that it works both ways.

Our functionality to respond as children is diminished when we take charge and put some things out of our lives. Our childish ways restrict us from operating in the Glory of God. Look at Apostle Paul and how he moved from his selfish ways and quickly matured into a leader of inspiration and revelation.

The Apostle Paul is direct when he says to put them away. He is talking about our ways. The childish ways that restrict us from reaching our destiny must be let go of. Simply look at Paul's life, and you will see that he put his childish ways away. Look at everything he let go of in his life.

Paul teaches us that we must identify what is childish in our lives. Unless we identify it each and every time, we will carry weight and issues that have nothing to do with our progress. I am saying that we must put away what we have been defending with our actions for so long. Prophet, this is a relationship issue!

What do we need to accomplish as an apostle or a prophet? The power of life and death is in the tongue and if you are not willing to honor that you will not grow. I am saying watch what you say about others, especially your peers.

Understanding will heal a multitude of issues. The term understanding is what we refer to as the truth that we stand on and under. The power of understanding is what will separate us from being a child to being an adult. This is how and why we must move forward from where we are at and not skip today for tomorrow.

The mentality of a mature prophet or a mature apostle is all about understanding. What we choose to understand or not understand is killing us as apostles or prophets.

When the apostles and prophets of this now generation learn how to pull themselves from where they started then and only then will we make a difference in the lives of those to whom they are sent to by God. This is when God will trust you with trouble; let me explain prophet.

CHAPTER 7

ARE YOU A PROPHET GOD TRUSTS WITH TROUBLE OR A PEER RELATIONSHIP?

Have you read *2 Corinthians 1:8?* Prophets, do not be ignorant, brethren of our trouble. Apostle Paul speaks about his experience in Asia. He says the men and him were burdened beyond measure. He goes on to say they were troubled above their strength, and they got to the point that they despaired even life. Apostle Paul is saying that He has been through the storm. He is saying that trials and tribulations will come, and sometimes, it can be almost too much to bear.

Apostle Paul also knew that satan and his imps have no intention of allowing you to be successful and at peace. Get this lesson. Apostle Paul is saying that in the midst of all this trouble when I thought I couldn't go on. God delivered me! He is saying God set him free. He is saying that God could trust him when the storm of life was raging. Are you walking in that type of relationship with God?

Prophet, can God trust you with trouble? Here are some questions to ponder:

1. Can God trust you when you are under attack?

2. Can He trust you when all hell is breaking loose around you?
3. Can God trust you when Satan decides to shoot a fiery dart at your Marriage or at your children?
4. Can He trust you when the bank says the check bounced?
5. Can He trust you when the boss doubles your work and not your pay?

Every Prophet of God will come under spiritual attack at one time or another. Many prophets are ignorant of where their trouble comes from. We will blame everyone, but God does not want us to be ignorant about anything. This is why we have His Word. The Holy Spirit is here to help us understand that Word.

The question is, can God trust you? God wants to know: will you stand and fight or will you cut and run? Will you, prophet, be the one that stands and watches, or will you take action? God wants you to know what to do when you are attacked and in a battle.

Look at Job, he lost 7,000 sheep, 3000 camels, 500 oxen, 500 she asses, and all his servants and even his children. *Job 42:12,* so the Lord blessed the latter end of Job more than his beginning. The Lord knew He could trust Job.

As a prophet, what happens when you get stressed out? There is a season for all things. *Ecclesiastes 9:12* clearly speaks of the time and prophets. We are like a fish taken in a cruel net. We are the birds caught in a snare. Evil is seeking the sons of men to snare us as evil falls upon us.

Ezekiel is called to be a prophet. God had a special task for him to do at a most difficult time in Jewish history. His service was to troubled people, the Jews who were away from their land.

The Jewish enemies had taken them to Babylon. The feelings among them were sadness and a lot of hopelessness. Think about this: the Jews felt that God did not care about them anymore.

Ezekiel's task was to come and declare God's message to them. Welcome to dealing with trouble. He is bringing a word to people dealing with trouble. Does this sound like you?

Ezekiel's task was to tell them they were in Babylon because they were being punished. Can you imagine the pressure upon Ezekiel? The issue is an extremely serious matter.

As the prophet of God, Ezekiel calls the Jews to live right. They were already upset, so his task was difficult. Ezekiel has a dual word of hope for the Jews. He tells them God has a plan for them, which is a prosperous future for them.

This is why prophets must learn from prophets. Dealing with a national problem and an awful personal experience, Ezekiel is called to what looks like a desperate and troublesome situation that no one would want to be called to alone. An unknown future was ahead of the Jews and they clearly felt that God was against them.

Look at Ezekiel's reactions to this situation; there is much we can learn about dealing with trouble.

1. God always reminds us that he never changes.

Despite the trouble or the type of trouble, God will always be the same. Our circumstances may change. Our attitude to life may change. But God is the same. Today, we are in the hot seat of times of trouble.

We, too, should remember that our circumstances may change. But God is always the same. Read *Malachi 3:6; Hebrews 1:11; 13:8; James 1:17* and *Revelation 1:4*.

We can feel that we have lost everything—all that really matters. This can happen when we are suffering and in pain. Sometimes, it may even seem that God has left us, too.

He knows all about our trouble. He has not left us alone in our world. He is with us in our suffering and despair. He also gives us all the power to deal with life.

This is true regardless of those problems. As a prophet, Ezekiel knew this, and his trust was in God. So God gave Ezekiel multiple visions for the people to minister to them.

Ezekiel's first vision fills his mind. It's a picture of God's throne. This is a special king's chair. It was like a very unusual vehicle. The picture language is clear. But it doesn't sound very easy (*Ezekiel 1:1-28*).

Ezekiel's vision was a special message, vital in any time of trouble. We need to remind ourselves and others in hard times that our God is sovereign, faithful, and never changes. He, being God, is still on the throne.

As prophets, we often make things worse for ourselves. When trouble comes, our reactions are wrong. There is resistance to God's authority. We become bitter and angry. We look at our awful troubles.

We, despite knowing better and simply ignoring the truth, seem to always find a way to compare and contrast and be in competition with other prophets and people as we see and ponder that others always seem to have success.

Let's look at trouble from another angle, which is called personal trouble *(Ezekiel 24:15-27)*. It is a very sad story about Ezekiel. What an awful day it must have been. His situation was very hard anyway.

God also told Ezekiel not to show his grief publicly when his precious wife died *(Ezekiel 24:15-18)*. Now, he knew that his wife would be dead by evening. But he still went to work in the morning. He accepted God's purpose. Can God trust you with trouble?

Look at this as the evening came. His very dear wife was dead. His first reaction to this news was vital. It would be a lesson to the Jews. They knew, and they were watching him; people know and are watching us daily as prophets to see how we handle certain situations in our lives. Prophet, get this: you are on the front line, which is the standard for all of us to aspire for.

As a prophet, God does not use only the words He gives us. He uses us as a model. He uses our actions. He uses our reactions to life's troubles. Prophet, can you be trusted with trouble? May I interject that this is about the relationship?

Ezekiel must not cry aloud. In other words, you would not see him posting all his personal business on Facebook or any other social media platform to vent or even get likes. He is mission-focused. The day after his wife's death was the same as usual. He did his work as a prophet *(Ezekiel 24:18)*.

So, he had a great chance to speak God's Word. His own sad loss became part of his message. It can be the same with our troubles. We can use our trouble to show truths about God. My question is, can you handle this?

It is true whatever our troubles may be. God is eager to lift us out of our pain and despair. He wants to give us new life. Look now at *Ezekiel 37:1-14*. Imagine now, the vision of the valley of dry bones. Let's now look at trouble from the valley perspective.

The Jews' present state was as bad as these bones in *Ezekiel 37:11*. The bones were' very dry' too (37:2). There was no hope. This is just how the Jews felt. They were in a foreign land. Everything was ruined. They felt depressed and hopeless. Someone needed to remind them about God's power. They needed to know about God's Spirit. They needed certainty about the future, too.

Better days were coming. They would return to their own land. God says: 'I have promised that I would do this and I will. I, the Lord, have spoken' (37:14). So, God used Ezekiel. He encouraged the people to hope. He made their trust and confidence in God stronger.

This vision refers to the Jews' national life at that time. But it has importance for us too today. We may feel very depressed. But God is sufficient for us. This is true whatever our personal pain and despair may be. He desires to make our love for him new again. He wants us to have stronger confidence and trust in him.

The prophet's incubation process is extraordinary, and it will never be anything less. You can simply expect a release of your personally held agenda almost always.

This is the standard operating procedure for receiving the purposes of the Giver. Imagine how Ezekiel felt, given his impossible, tough assignment and the loss of his wife, yet he continued.

Then there is Mary, who dreamed of having multiple sons. The purpose of God required that she become mother to Jesus. How about Hannah? She was tormented and abused en route to be the mother to the prophet Samuel. Samuel would become the prophet that God hand-chosen to bring His people back to Him.

Of all the judges, there is Prophetess Deborah. She was chosen to give God's Word to His people. She was known as the psalm tree prophet. Prophetess Deborah was so highly respected that the general named Barak was scared to lead his army into battle without her. Can you see that because of her position, she has inherited trouble?

She had proven trustworthy to God and the people. Deborah was available for God to use her to encourage an army to rise up against Israel's oppressors. This is how God employs his prophets in times of trouble to accomplish His purposes. God uses these kinds of lives to incubate the extraordinary.

Every prophet, no matter who you are, you will experience these seasons. Seasons when your best seems so small in wake of the trouble around your life. The prophet can expect experiences filled with storms and inexplicable difficulty.

Prophets, we can be assured that God sees our faithfulness and He knows our hearts. Like His prophets, and even the examples of Mary and Hannah, we must prove trustworthy. We must face our fears like Prophetess Deborah or Jael.

God tells His prophets to do things that would be difficult for anyone. This is part of the message we bring. For example, God told Jeremiah not to marry and he must not attend funerals, feasts or weddings *(Jeremiah 16: 1-9)*. Why did God do this?

Faith that can't be tested is faith that can't be trusted. There will always be very difficult events in the personal lives of prophets. The truth is sometimes you will suffer things in public.

Welcome to the now generation world you live in Prophet, and you have been assigned to. The question I put before you again, can you be trusted with trouble, prophet? Are you in the right relationship to not mock and disrespect your peer prophets?

CHAPTER 8

DISRESPECT AND MOCKING OF A PROPHET

Now, let's define the word Prophet. They are not just a mere speaker but a messenger who carries God's divine authority. We can also say the prophet is one through whom God's holy will is expressed. The prophet is a person chosen by God to pass on His message. This divine authority is not to be taken lightly; disrespecting God or His prophets is a grave offense.

So when a prophet is mocked or disrespected, it is not just a casual act but a serious offense because it is a direct reflection on God! This includes churches, people in general, and, yes, prophetic peers. The gravity of this offense cannot be overstated.

Respecting prophets is not a matter of personal preference. Respect always requires a level of discernment that many lack. This discernment is not just about recognizing the gift, but understanding and acknowledging the divine authority and message they carry. It is a crucial aspect of our faith.

Let's get started with what we are to understand about mocking. Mock means to act hypocritically. Have you ever been or had a person who makes pretenses or professions about a prophet or a person? To make a mockery of a prophet is to be hypocritical and make false, unsubstantiated claims and representations that are not true.

Be honest. Have you ever done this because you did not know that prophet or you heard something about that prophet? The reality of the interrelationship among prophets should mean something.

I am not a behavior expert, but sometimes we see them, meaning peer prophets, and we don't like how they are dressed. Sometimes, we are so petty as to evaluate their hair and makeup.

We often evaluate by fashion, gossip, and personality. This can include making fun of a prophet's appearance or personal habits.

However, we should utilize the Spirit of prophetic discernment, which is the ability to perceive and understand the divine will and message. Prophetic discernment is not about judging a prophet based on superficial traits, but about recognizing and respecting the divine authority they carry.

Within our circles, we mock and pretend to love and serve God when we are not. Mocking authorizes us to act falsely, insincerely, and especially hypocritically in our professions.

We pretend to obey God, saying we love, serve, and worship Him when we do not. Mocking, in a nutshell, is insincerity, anything that is only pretense and does not represent the state of the heart.

Then we have the nerve to wonder why our relationships within the prophetic are seemly in and out of the toilet. The term to mock, in ordinary language, is a term of dishonor and disrespect. This means that God is mocked by not being honored. To mock a prophet is not just to make fun of them, but to dishonor the divine authority they carry. Prophet, this is serious business.

The Bible says, "Our God is not and will not be mocked; what a man soweth, he will reap." The prophet of today has to understand and obey God's Word. This is how we show that we respect and honor His Word.

When we don't make time or pay attention when His Word is being read, we disrespect God and His Word. This is one of the most prevalent examples of disrespect and mockery we see as prophets and within our ranks. Yes, this will vary by culture, but the truth is the truth.

Unless we, the prophets, are really in an obedient state of mind and in the true spirit of devotion to His service, we mock God by the very fact of coming to His house for any other reason.

In *Psalm 105:15,* God speaks of Israel and the prophets assigned there. Also, look at verse 14: "God has suffered no man to do them wrong, and the question is, who are they?"

We have all heard of the prophets: "Touch not mine anointed; we are His anointed ones whom He has directed to do no harm." Let me point out that the word anointing refers to the inaugural ceremony of priests. In the Old Testament, priests were anointed with oil. This anointing was representative of the Holy Spirit.

This means that priests were set aside for the divine purposes of God. Stay with me here. The Holy Spirit is the anointing of priests. This is what was poured out upon all in this new royal priesthood. History tells us that there was a change of priesthood, from the Levitical priesthood. The change was to the order of Melchizedek, a royal priesthood (*Hebrews 7:11*). Now here is where we see the abuse of prophets.

In the world today and as was in the royal priesthood, we see the brash and meddling hands and tactics that have stoned the prophets physically and spiritually. We can't deny there is a prevailing attitude in religious circles, even in some Bible-believing churches and circles, that it is okay to ridicule and insult God's prophets. Yes, we are doing them harm.

Let's look at *2 Kings 2:23-24*. We see Elisha curse a group of men who are youths. They were disrespecting him as they called him bald head, as they found his baldness to be a joke.

Can you imagine a group of kids cursing and disrespecting Elisha? I often wonder where they got the idea to curse God's prophets. Let's think about this for a moment. Could it be they heard their parents?

Maybe a better question is why you and I disrespect the prophet of God today, because we see they may be different from us. What is sad is that it works both ways. Have you ever considered this prophet?

Let's think about this as your son is following Elisha up to Bethel. He is walking, tending to his business and your son says to Elisha, "hey baldhead" and he and others keep saying this to God's prophet.

I must tell you that Elisha is human, and he has a tolerance level, like you and I do. Scripture says he turned around. He now looks at them and calls a curse on them. Can you imagine this.?

Not one but two bears came out of the woods. We see a group of youth who are mauled. Prophet consider what God did. There is not one but two huge bears that maul a group of young men for making fun of one of His prophets. A group of men assembled for the sole purpose of mocking a prophet of God.

Read this carefully. What is the difference today when we see Christians, who profess Christ and we see them mocking the seers and prophets of God? Today to add salt to the wound, is two central facts.

The first fact is so many of today's prophets do not receive any formal training in their gift or in the basic prophetic protocol. The second fact is that so many prophets have felt entitled because they have a gift and the gift has been misused and disrespected by many pastors, bishops and yes apostles and other prophets.

Consider an additional fact. It is very hard to have a good relationship with someone who feels disrespected and insulted. Let's put *2 Kings 2:23-24* in summary. It is a record of misplaced relationships that result in a totally insulting demonstration against one of God's prophets.

What I am saying here is simple, but often abused by those who fail to understand the logic of how God sees this issue. He is in a relationship with His prophets and when you insult and disrespect His servants, you must understand what is next.

The penalty was clear for the young men. They were punished in a justified way for what they did to Elisha. I am saying what they did to His prophet was to do it to God Himself. The seriousness of the crime is clear, and we see it demonstrated in the punishment. The judgment was, and the judgment is to all those who would scorn the prophets of the Lord.

Prophets, do we really understand we can control the degree to which people persist in being disrespectful? Their behavior and attitude rest primarily in how we respond as prophets of this new generation.

Over and over so often, we have heard people in the Body of Christ disrespect and mock prophets and then come into the prophet's face wanting a prophetic word or a prophetic blessing.

Let's understand it is impossible to force people to be respectful. What is possible is that we educate people about our lives for Christ, that respectful behavior will bless them, and disrespectful behavior will not serve them.

Prophets, your attitude and philosophy are essential ingredients. Your actions and how you conduct yourself will change or modify people's actions and words concerning disrespect, and this is how you must expend the energy to teach them that their attitude has costs. Welcome to kingdom relationship building.

Generally, in the world, there are built-in solutions for disrespect. Let's say you disrespect your boss; they will lose their job, but that's simple. Now, what if they treat their customers with disrespect? Do not expect to see those customers back.

Also, it is an issue because it is not a customer, which means no profit. Also, have you considered that by being disrespectful and rude to your friends, you can generally expect to lose them as quality friends?

The key thing here is loss. The same is true for the prophetic. Those prophets whom you disrespect, you lose. What makes this so critical is that they lose from God. So, prophet, understand that disrespectful behavior is not worth your attention.

Consider these four facts. Number one is that the world as a whole will not invest in disrespect. Number two is that good friends will not invest their energy into disrespectful peers, especially in the prophetic. Number three is that employers do not invest in disrespect. Number four is that specialty schools do not invest in disrespect.

Prophets must learn that teaching respect requires more from them than the people who disrespect them. It is essential to have the right attitude and perspective.

Know this fact prophet, you cannot force compliance nor can you force respect, or behavior. Your focus must be on learning how to accept and send appropriate interactions. This is how new people who don't understand your gift may get to know you better.

2 Kings 5, as Naaman wanted to bless Elisha, would not accept his offering. Why? Because of his disrespect and bad attitude toward God's Word. It is not worthy of your energy, prophets.

Moses demonstrates this to us in *Numbers 12:1-2, 4-9,* where we see, "And Miriam and Aaron are two prophets who spake against Moses. They were family also. They did this because of the Ethiopian woman whom Moses had married.

God heard how they spoke disrespectfully of Moses and He calls them out. Then they were afraid to speak against Moses? Look at God's anger against them, and He departed.

"Miriam became leprous." Aaron now cries out to God and Moses about how foolish Miriam is, and He has spoken. Miriam is most likely the instigator in this, and the complaints in verses 1 and 2 are different. Aaron is a follower! Isn't that the way it usually happens?

It is difficult to imagine a more diverse group of personalities than the prophets. There is no indication that God chose men of any particular kind of background, personality, talent, or education. He chooses those he can use best at the moment, or the one He could best prepare for future service.

Prophets, as we attempt to do what God has called us to do, learn how Paul reveals something of the problem that he faced in his attempt to reach as many persons as possible in his generation. Read *1 Corinthians 9:19-22*. Allow me to para phase."

For though I be free from all men, yet have I made myself as a servant unto all. The object is to gain more. He sees himself as being all things to all men that some might be saved. Did you not know he did not expect all of them to be saved? This is a critical problem we have today as we think everybody is going to accept us. The reality is that they won't.

A message to go to every nation's tongue and people must not be built in a restricted manner. Many minds, talents, personalities, environments, and lines of activity must lend their influence to make the message appealing to so wide a field. Prophets understand why difficult people are the norm you will face in your life as a prophet.

Prophets, do you respect God? When prophets don't respect God, we open up ourselves to the spirit of disrespect. The word "respect" means to feel or show deferential regard for or to esteem. It is to avoid violation of or interference with God, who demands our respect.

God's name should be feared in the sense that He should be regarded with high esteem, and He should be revered above all else. When either we as prophets or people show little or no respect for His messenger, who is His representative, you have disrespected God.

The last book of the Old Testament is credited to Malachi (which means "my messenger"). Look at *Malachi 1:6- 8* and the prophet; you will see the honor demonstrated. See that a son will honor his father and a servant of his master. Read this as God speaks to the priests who say they honor Him but do not.

The priests asked, "In what way God did we disrespect you?" God speaks in numerous ways to the priest. He says you have defiled food on my altar, and then you have the nerve to offer the blind as a sacrifice.

Prophet, would God be pleased with you? Would He accept you favorably? The Lord of Hosts is asking. When we don't offer God our best, we offend Him.

The priests were going through the motions in regard to worshipping God. They were not sincere in offering the required sacrifices to God. They truly showed contempt for God by their actions. Consider what the above scripture says, prophets as we all need to check ourselves before we check others.

A son honors his father and a servant his master – This is typical behavior of humans. The son honors his father, and a servant will honor his master. Similarly, an employee will honor his employer, and an athlete will honor his coach. We honor those in authority over us. However, the Jews did not show this typical respect and honor for God. They showed contempt for God.

If then I am the Father, Where is my honor? – God is the father and master, and yet He was not respected as one would respect a father or master here on earth. Of course, those who are not Christians do not respect God, but even those who call themselves Christians show contempt for God in their lifestyles and various activities.

The Malachi told the priests that they despised God through their sacrifices. They were offering things to God that were defiled. They were offering blind, maimed, or otherwise unacceptable sacrifices to God. They were in essence giving God their rejects. Look at *Deuteronomy 15:21.* We see God make a valid point by asking if their governors would accept such sacrifices.

Should we give to God if there is a deficit or a serious defect? Scripture says, you shall not sacrifice it to the Lord your God. *Matthew 6:33* says, "But seek first the kingdom of God and His righteousness, and all these things shall be added to you."

Do we really hold God in enough high esteem to seek His kingdom first? The word first here refers to priority or importance. In other words, God and His kingdom should be the number one priority in our lives. Is it?

We put so many other things over and above seeking the Lord God. The fact of the matter is that He is simply not important enough to us. We don't respect Him the way we should. How often do we talk to God? How often do we spend time in communion with Him?

Look at *Matthew 13:22.* It is critical as the Word says he. Let's identify who the prophet is. It is you and I. We are the ones who received seed among the thorns. Despite what is happening, we are trusting God.

We are the ones who hear the word. Question for you? Do we hear the word or are we caught up so much with the cares of this world and the deceitfulness of riches? These are the things that choke the Word, and he becomes unfruitful.

The focused prophet is one who understands that the things that bombard us in life cause us to lose focus on the very thing that would help us cope with those things. The job, children, bills, hobbies, habits, etc, all get in the way and demand our respect for them more than God.

These things are so much a part of the world that we operate in, namely the physical world. God is Spirit and so He will not be to us as material things are and yet He is just as real and more. God is eternal and these things are only for a short while.

Read *Malachi 1:10-11*. What this says is, "Who has enough nerve to close the church so that you wouldn't come worship me in vain?" The Jews were wasting their time in their worship activities.

It would have been just as effective to not offer the sacrifices. Their sacrifices were not accepted by God so there was really no need for the priests to offer them. God said that His name (He) would be great among the Gentiles.

This is important because the gentile's perspective of God will surely be influenced by what they see those who call themselves God people do in regard to worship, praise, and reverence of God. Why should they come to respect God if we don't show respect for God?

Prophets, again our conduct has to be Godly, not trying to make people think you are holy, but be a standard of the God that you serve. Have a foundation. Therefore, respect and disrespect are ministries to those who are not part of God's family.

It all comes down to simply fearing (revering) God and doing what He says. Nothing else is as important as our relationship with God. Nothing is therefore more important than God and His Word. We should therefore respect God because of who He is.

Prophet, respect God in Word and deed. Make it a habit to respect God by the things that you do and not just by the things that you say. Make your homage to church each Sunday meaningful and not just a religious obligation. Start by praying to God and establishing a real relationship with Him even though you cannot see or feel Him physically.

Develop a lasting relationship with God that would transcend any situation here on earth. The Prophet Ezekiel is a prime example. What kind of relationship would you require with God to have a hard conversation? I am talking about what if God told you your spouse would die, but He needed you to go on assignment for him?

Prophet, you must draw closer to God, and you will experience God as He will draw near to you. Make God the priority in your life, and remember to respect and honor at all times.

CHAPTER 9

PROPHETS HAVING DIFFICULT CONVERSATIONS WITH GOD

I am going to assume you are a prophet or at least you love God. Along this walk, we will have a difficult conversation with God.

We have difficult conversations with each other or with those whom we serve. These conversations are about sharing different perspectives and seeking divine guidance and understanding our roles in God's plan.

This chapter will discuss and examine our relationships and how they are affected by our difficult conversations with God. Have you ever had a difficult talk with God?

Did you know that sharing different perspectives can build mutual understanding and develop respect? We should be alert to our different cultures, customs, and traditions. Respecting our differences will go a long way in helping us have difficult conversations.

It is no secret that difficult conversations can occur in any situation. The prophet of God may have needs/wants, opinions, or perceptions that are different and diverse among all involved parties.

This is why we discussed anger in previous chapters as feelings often characterized by fear, frustration, and conflict.

Most people are reluctant to open a difficult conversation out of fear of the consequences. Typically, when and if the conversation occurs, the parties think and feel much more than they say.

It's important to remember that difficult conversations with God can be transformative. They can strengthen our relationships, alleviate stress, and prevent resentment and conflict. Consider the potential for growth and enlightenment in these conversations with God.

Question to ask yourself? Have you ever had a difficult conversation with God? What happens when a prophet has a difficult conversation with God? What happens when God directs you to do something, and you know it will be difficult?

You know it will be hard and you know it will cost you. What do you do when you have to make a decision on something God has told you to do and you are hesitant to do it?

Consider that God has entrusted you with a difficult assignment following a challenging conversation. Despite your doubts and apprehensions, it's crucial to remember that God knows your capabilities better than you do. Trusting in His plan is key to navigating these difficult conversations.

Ezekiel 24:15-27 is the saga of the Prophet Ezekiel. Ezekiel is a married man and he is also God's prophet.

God has a mission for him, and God tells him that your wife, whom you love, will be dead before you complete your mission. What would be your mindset if you had this conversation with God?

God tells him that he will not be able to mourn, and he is to put on his clothes and go forth in the assignment he has with Israel. Notice that God tells him not to eat the bread of man's sorrow, meaning he should not dwell on his personal grief but focus on the mission.

So you want to be God's prophet. How difficult would a conversation be with you? Two things you should notice here that will help you understand why this is a difficult conversation with God. The first is that Ezekiel's mission was for the people to repent and return to God. The mission was bigger than Ezekiel's personal issue.

While this was the objective, the second reason elevates the personal burden of the Prophet Ezekiel. He is sent by God to do a work that demonstrates the cost of serving God.

Prophet, you must know that to serve God there is a cost. There is a real relationship with God being demonstrated here.

To serve God and serve as a prophet, there is an added burden that you need to understand and be prepared for. Imagine if you were Ezekiel, and God spoke to you and declared that I have an assignment for you and that I will take away your ability to mourn. Your loved one will no longer be a part of your life.

Do you love God enough to understand that life does not stop for you to hurt or for your pain? Life goes on. Now if that sounds cold and heartless to you let me urge you to read and understand that Ezekiel was committed and he had to go forth.

Ezekiel is human, and his ability to mourn is gone. Sure, we can assume that he has to think about the fact that he is going out on the battlefield for God, and he is losing his wife on the same day. We do know that he did not mourn, and he was fully obedient to God's directive.

What separates Ezekiel from other prophets? What separates Ezekiel from you? Do you understand that God is not concerned with comfort; he is concerned with your development?

Since God has no respect of person it could be you who God gives a difficult task and your conversation with God is difficult because you know what it will cost you. Being God's prophet means being a vessel for His will, even when it's difficult or painful.

So what do we see in Ezekiel's life that we can draw from? A close look at Ezekiel reveals a rigid self-discipline. We also see a passion for God as he is willing to be an example for the people to observe.

Can God have a difficult conversation with you and can you be counted on to process it and obey the assignment? Having a difficult conversation with God can be a challenging experience. Are you able to process your pain and still serve God?

In *Exodus 3* we see Moses and he has a difficult conversation with God. He is called to service and he feels he is unworthy. Simply put, Moses is scared and intimidated by the task given by God.

Have you ever been there? 40 years in the wilderness and now God calls him to bring a nation of people out of a nation. The task is overwhelming to Moses and he is reluctant to move forward. His dialogue with God reveals much about his mindset.

Can you see Moses? He has been stripped of his pride and his Egyptian ways in the wilderness. He has a stuttering problem. God is assigning Moses to do something that Moses does not have the faith to do. Now how difficult does that sound to you? Even the great Moses gets his introduction as God's prophet, as he is welcomed to the prophetic.

Exodus 4 reflects the character of Moses, a figure we can all relate to. He pleads with God, but God reassures him that He will be with him, dispelling any fear or anxiety.

Moses' journey is a testament, to having a difficult conversation with God. Moses is challenged to move in the power of faith in overcoming fear. This is a lesson we can all learn from when faced with God's assignments.

What will you do when God gives you an assignment that you are trying to see and you can't because God, like he did with Moses, did not intend for Moses to see it? This was about building the faith of his Prophet. Can you trust God in this process?

You need to see this in your life. You can't be a prophet and not have a difficult conversation with God. The reality is that as a prophet you will have difficult conversations with God and you must be able to trust God in His purpose to engage you with such a conversation.

So what do you do and how do you prepare yourself prophet? There are three things you should be able to do constantly.

1. You should be able to prepare yourself spiritually. Take time to pray and invite God to mediate on the conflict and submit your emotions to Him. Always use the word of God. The men-

tality of getting the word will help you prepare for a difficult conversation and difficult God given task.

2. Always be in touch with your motives. Check them. Prophet have you asked yourself why God is having this difficult conversation with you? Do you believe that God has His faith within you to accomplish what He wants to do in your life?

Does the difficult conversation encourage you? Do you seek to honor God and build a stronger relationship with Him, or are you motivated by selfish desires?

3. When God has a difficult conversation with you, do you demonstrate God's love? In other words, are you humble? Do you acknowledge God's hand at work in your life and be willing to put your pride to death?

The prophet needs to learn that listening actively is the way to ensure you hear clearly the point that God is making in your life. Does the conversation you have with God seek your reconciliation?

Do you build a stronger relationship with God with the difficult assignments you have gotten from HIm? How does your relationship with God and others affect you as you have difficult conversations with God?

Remember that having a difficult conversation with God can be a growth opportunity and a chance to deepen your faith. With prayer, preparation, and a willingness to listen and show love, you learn to navigate a difficult conversation with God with grace and humility.

CHAPTER 10

PROPHETS IN A DRY LAND OR A DRY SEASON

Prophet, as we continue to discuss relationships, let us read *Isaiah 24:1-5*. The Word says the Lord is going to lay waste on the earth. He will devastate it, ruin its face, and scatter the people upon it. The earth will be completely laid waste.

What is defiling the earth? The answer is people. The people who have disobeyed the laws and violated the statutes are the ones who have broken the everlasting covenant. We are the messengers of hope to restore this. As we look at our relationship with God, what do we see?

The word describes the earth, as a symbol of the promised land of Palestine that had become defiled due to the disobedience of God's chosen people. They had violated the Law, and now they would reap the retribution of God.

The Valley of Dry Bones, a vision given to the Prophet Ezekiel more than 2500 years ago, remains a poignant question for us today. Can these dry bones live? That question echoes in the hearts of prophets in every generation, including ours.

The vision aims to revive the flagging spirits of God's elect both now and then. The blight of doubt wilts and withers lives that were once lovely and fragrant as roses. Churches that once budded and flourished in the early rains become parched by the discouragement that prevents the latter rains.

Relationships conceived in love and brought through faith may die in cynicism and despair. Now, everything is in a dry land. Here is where we now discuss the prophet in a dry land and why they are there.

First and foremost, it's important to understand that being in a spiritually dry place isn't necessarily negative unless it's a result of sin. When we knowingly commit a sin, God may withhold His fellowship from us.

Here we feel a distance between the Lord and ourselves. So often, it is so painful. As prophets, we must understand the call to repentance. This is a powerful tool to bridge the gap and restore our spiritual vitality.

We should remember that being in a dry land doesn't mean the Lord is abandoning us or that He doesn't love us. If anything, it's a demonstration of His love. He allows us to feel the broken fellowship because it moves us to repentance. His love is a constant, even in our driest times. I am talking about relationship building.

I wish I could count the times that the prophet will find themselves in a dry land. So often it is for a specific time that the Lord wants us to go through. Can your relationship handle a time of testing and of preparation as a prophet?

The Lord allows us to be tested to refine our faith. This understanding can motivate us to stay focused and endure the dryness, knowing that it's part of our preparation.

Consider our salvation is dependent on the feeling of fellowship with the Lord; is it rooted in our unwavering trust in Jesus, God in flesh *(John 1:1, 14)*, as our Savior and Lord? Our justification is by faith *(Rom. 5:1)*, and our assurance of salvation is found in faith, not in feeling. Do you mean it when you say that the just shall live by faith? Do we even consider ourselves as being the just *(Hab. 2:4)?*

The fact is that the Lord can use a prophet spiritually in a dry land to cause us to examine what or who our faith is in because our feelings can deceive us *(Jer. 17:9)*.

Dry lands can also be a time of preparation. Every prophet who was used mightily of God had to go through a desert time. This includes Moses, Elijah, Elisha, Joseph, and others. Being alone in a dry land, where all it seems we do is wait, want, and pray is an experience of being examined.

The opportunity of such a test is one of strength and refinement. When this test or exam is completed, the thing that we have been in training for comes upon our lives.

The prophet's preparation is one of hardship, sorrow, and pain. This is the plan of God. This is the building of your relationship with God and the ability to impart into other prophets and people.

Prophet, remember, that God has not chosen you to be a trophy on a shelf. We are His prophets. We are His instruments in His hands. What we have as experiences prepares us to be used in the world for His glory.

To be used by God requires that we are able to be used. We are able to be sent. We are able to be trusted by God, despite what we see and feel. Prophet, please do not despise the time of spiritual dryness; it is a time of preparation.

Every now generation prophet should prepare themselves for dry seasons. I want to discuss things you need to do as you find yourself in Dryland. You will find that this is all about relationships, prophet.

1. Ask God to reveal any unconfessed sins of which you have not repented. This is critical. Understand that if God reveals anything to you, confess and repent. Do not hesitate to confess and repent.
2. Second, you must read your Word regularly.
3. Third, you must pray regularly.
4. Trust God through the test. Remember, this is about relationships. Prophetic relationships are always tough to build for a prophet, but we must remember that God loves us and will never forsake us.

This is how we process our faith into maturity and trust. Our faith is perfected, our character improves, and our walk strengthens. We are prepared for the tasks ahead that the Lord has called us to encounter.

A dry land can be defined as any one of the following:

- Houses with pastors who are controlling, manipulating and threatened by the Prophetic gift to include healing and deliverance gifts.
- Churches and ministries that are hostile to anything that God is ushering in.

- A region that is hostile to the apostolic and prophetic move of God.
- A church that does not respect the prophetic gifts, prophets, or the 5 Fold ministry.
- A troubled or hostile home or marriage that is controlling.
- Relationships that you are in that do not understand the calling upon your life and can't nurture or bring you to maturity.
- A place of ignorance and resistance to the truth of God's Word.
- A place where there is a lack of repentance and fasting.
- On a personal level, when you are stuck, dormant, dry, or bound in sin.
- On a personal level, when you do not know your purpose or destiny.

What should the prophet do in this situation?

1. Develop your personal and intimate relationship with God by developing your prayer life with Intercession and fasting.
2. Get to prophetic watering holes such as schools, conferences, and revivals. They will help prepare you for your calling.
3. Study, study, and study. This will draw your affection back to God.
4. Get connected to a genuine prophetic company.
5. Ask God for a prophetic mentor in the gifting's upon your life.
6. Get the training and continue training. The more the better.
7. Develop a life of journaling while keeping a record of God's instructions (Record your dreams and visions).
8. Review and pray through your personal prophetic words. Hold onto the word you are given.
9. Invest in yourself. Build a media library of selected materials on your gift.
10. Don't underestimate the power of incubation and impartation. You are there for a reason.

11. Understand that timing is key. Do not try to make your own way before you're ready, which means someone will identify you as God leads them. Follow God's plan. It is so much better for you.
12. Learn how, through and by the Word of God, you war with the demonic strongholds in your area. Don't allow them to rule over you!
13. Understand Ezekiel 37 is the key! Prophesy to a dry land and your situation!
14. Don't be afraid to use your prophetic gift, witness, and evangelize for Christ.
15. Be obedient. Get your personal deliverance from the demonic spirits that rule your region and be obedient to the Spirit of God.

The warfare in a dry land or season is serious business with a purpose. When a prophet finds themselves in dry land or season you need to understand that there are prophetic principles of wealth and prosperity that need to be activated to bring a harvest. The enemy fights us so bad in the arena of finances that we shy away or stop pursuing what God has for us.

Our work in a dry land or season is needed to mature us to achieve financial stability in ministry. Let us discuss this because this is the one area where we will be tested the most and exposed greatly. The employment of the following principles is needed to employ the prophet to improve the relationship with God and their peers.

1. Without faith you can never access prophetic money and prosperity. Prophetic money starts in the faith realm, not your bank account. The same is true of prophetic wealth and prophetic Health. Be advised that this is real faith and real work within oneself.

2. Understand that prophetic words on finance come with great warfare. Demonic assignments are released to stop the flow. The enemy tries to dry up all financial streams as a siege method.
3. The timing of God and your obedience is key to any prophetic word. Your faith sets the stage for the future generations that will come after you. They will learn from you!
4. Impatience is the enemy of the prophetic utterance. Prophecy signals that God has a plan for your benefit. The prophetic word concerning finances is always hindered by being lazy and stingy.
5. If you are receiving multiple prophetic word on wealth, understand that much given will require much. You must begin to prepare yourself to handle the wealth with the resources you have.
6. A lack of maturity will put a hold on prophetic releases, especially in dealing with wealth and prosperity.
7. As a prophet, using your ability to bless others will keep your gate open and destroy the works of the enemy to block your blessings.
8. Guard yourself against unbelief. The enemy will have you think that the prophetic word of God is a lie and that type of thinking will put a hold on prosperity until someone has the faith to possess it!
9. Don't waste time! Your most valuable asset is time! Successful people in any endeavor guard their time. At the end of the day, what have you done today to build your ministry? Too many prophets go through life with nothing produced because they allow people, friends, and others to steal their time.

This robs them of future potential. Until you identify your time wasters and remove them, you won't grow or experience prosperity. You can't replace lost time.

10. Work to create a continuous prophetic environment that will be the foundation for miraculous releases.
11. Be willing to grow up and mature in all areas of your life especially the financial arena. If you're scared to give that is a contagious spirit. When you don't invest in your ministry, do not expect anyone else to. When prophets mature in the financial arena, they are ready to receive the fullness of God's Word in that area as well as in any area of prosperity.
12. Work to seek the Kingdom of God and His righteousness. This is the key to overthrowing the evil works of the enemy. Righteousness is a weapon of warfare that will outlive unrighteousness.

The issue of a dry land or season is part of the process of losing your normalcy as a prophet. We have to explore the relationship of the prophet operating in a different type of normal.

CHAPTER 11

LOSING YOUR NORMALCY AS A PROPHET

God's gifts are given to His prophets to empower them to bless others. Sometimes, you will encourage and give life-giving words to others. Sometimes, the gift of teaching will be activated upon you. Sometimes deliverance will show up.

The reality is that our prophetic gifts are diverse and given for the benefit of others. If you're a prophet, God has given you gifts.

When God uses a prophet who has undergone a maturing process, you can discern that the prophet knows how to steward their gifts effectively. This type of stewardship involves a significant investment of time, energy, and enthusiasm for the good of others and, most of all, the glory of God.

These identifying factors distinguish a prophet's life from what is considered 'normal.' Did you notice that I am talking about a prophet who has been through some type of dry season, a period of spiritual growth and refinement to even reach this point in their life?

Because prophets are gifted, they may experience what looks to be an early success with little or no failure, while others may outwardly struggle. The prophet may see the rapid advancement of their gift, and people may be blessed and empowered.

This is why the prophet must be careful and seek God. The prophetic leadership of that prophet should warn that prophet to be humble and hungry. The season of signs and wonders comes with a cost.

This is why the application of how the prophet handles being gifted is one of the ultimately strongest factors that determines how truly successful a prophet becomes. This is what will separate prophets from within the prophetic spectrum.

The question is raised: Have you worked hard or struggled to employ your skills to maximize your gifts?

These prophets often find that their inborn or natural talent is no longer sufficient to be successful. This is humbling, and things that were easy to them now are not.

Many prophets never learn the skills of godly success because they never build a relationship with God or his Godly, specifically directed peers who He sends and can help them. They lose their normalcy as emerging prophets and remain lost.

What is normalcy in a prophet's life? Normalcy is a condition that has a typical way of functioning. Those functions can have standard limits. Prophetic skills are not simply a result of inborn or natural talent but are birthed through chaos, hard work, persistence, patience, perseverance, and discipline. This is the prophetic arc process.

These are not new terms. These skills are developed so that you do not become normal. Prophetic success, however, is not just about achieving conventional success.

The issue here is about achieving a 'godly success,' which may require the prophet to sacrifice their 'normal' life. Allow me to welcome a hand full of you to losing your normalcy as a prophet.

Let me explain, as each culture will have its own unique way of expressing this. As a prophet, you become a target of criticism by peers, family, and even by people you may have never known.

Your ability to do the work will make you a target of those who seek to use you. But remember, it's in these moments of criticism and doubt that your perseverance as a prophet is truly tested. It's your resilience that will carry you through when everything in your world is not normal.

Some people will want you for the employment of your gifts; some will want you for your covenant connections, and others for your unique ability to operate in the fullness of what God has simply called you to do. Know those who you labor with.

Peers and people will often want to exploit your loss of normalcy for their own gain. The reality of everyone having an opinion of you becomes all too real. They will use your visibility as a prophet to make assumptions about you. Get used to it, as it will happen if you do good or bad.

This is especially true in significant relationships for prophets, such as with their parents, siblings, friends, and bosses, and especially in intimate interactions with peer prophets.

Have you considered the value of your peer prophetic relationships lately? They are your support system, sounding board, and refuge in times of testing or trial. You must understand why people are in your life. Is it a season or a reason?

Will you also consider that opportunities arise when a prophet becomes known? Keep in mind that not all of these opportunities may be of God, especially when you look into any specific culture's current view of reality.

While the prophet may see their gift as an asset, remember you are always in a position with a bullseye on you. Prophet because you are high profile, are a target for what is viewed as moral or, in some's opinion, immoral.

Let me ask a crazy question. Who are you in a relationship with to speak with and bounce ideas off, even as you pray daily? The reality of the loss of normalcy can hit a prophet really hard. Accomplishing great things is excellent, but at the same time, you may be dealing with agony.

You are subjected to the opinions and norms of those who do not know you. All this happens again because of your gift and the opportunity it affords you as a prophet.

Imagine the life of Moses. He is sent to represent God. God has sent him to free the children of Egypt from bondage. To some, Moses is viewed as a savior, a God himself, but he is also considered a failure. He is looked at, as being selfish and leads the people into a worse situation than they were already in as they were trying to escape. Can you imagine the chaos?

Do you remember Moses in *Exodus 2:11-15* as he kills a man and runs to exile? Sure, he has spent forty years in the wilderness. Do you think anyone remembers him? Or maybe they heard of him. The reality of the ancient society gossip line is just as real as social media is today. You can't doubt that someone may have remembered him, whether they were Egyptians or Israelites.

These are the same folks you know today who won't let go of what happened to you or what you did and now forty-four years later, they are still talking about it. Have you ever seen a family member mad for years over something they will not forget?

What is funny is that the same people who are critical of Moses are the very ones who are running to him, every time they are scared and frightened. This is classic and for all practical purposes, Moses has now lost his sense of normalcy.

Being gifted is an overrated contributor to success. The most significant predictor of success for the prophet is answering the question, "Is the prophet ready for the hard work and dedication needed for success?"

Can you imagine how hard it was for Moses to return to the palace despite his setbacks and failures in the past? Moses, whom God developed in the wilderness, was gifted, but was he successful? Moses had to be willing to lose the sense of normalcy in his daily life.

He had been developed in the wilderness, and now God tests him to see if he can be successful. Can you see the relationship connection he had to have with God to be used by God in that type of experience?

Moses was gifted but his success was in fulfilling the mission of God upon his life. He was to deliver the children of Israel and lead them to the reality of God. Remember the 10 commandments on the mountain?

In this season, are you willing to let go of your normal and become a success in God? Remember this: there is a difference between a successful prophet and a gifted prophet.

What we must understand is that both will experience a loss of normalcy. The extent to which this happens in either prophet's life is based on maturity, character, how they pursue their calling, and the impact they make.

Let's look at a gifted prophet. There is no doubt they possess an innate ability to receive and communicate divine revelations. The focus of a gifted prophet is being able to deliver accurate messages and revelations. The effectiveness of a gifted prophet is often limited by spiritual maturity or recognition they seek from and by others, especially their peers.

The successful prophet is a prophet who learns how to combine gifting with developed character, wisdom, and, most of all, faith. The successful prophet will trust and gain the trust of authorities through consistent alignment with God's purposes.

The successful prophet is known for humility, accuracy, and alignment with God's purposes. This type of prophet often influences broader communities of leaders than the simply gifted prophet.

The relationships of prophetic leaders within the prophetic community are often the result of a loss of normalcy for both parties. The loss of normalcy has become normal in their lives.

Prophets need to develop relationships of content and character because the prophet will always be in the spotlight as the messenger of God and thus can't hide.

While exploring our differences, we must accept that we jointly lose a sense of normalcy. How we handle ourselves is the key to understanding that our relationships are critical to our success.

We can't continue to allow recognition and media attention to define us. We must learn to foster peace, love, and justice and have the capacity to align with God's purposes.

In summary, while being gifted is a foundation, the success of the prophet totally requires character development, faithfulness, and effective stewardship of the prophetic calling. This is why we lose a sense of normalcy; we do change as we learn how to live by a more sure word. Keep reading, and I will explain this.

CHAPTER 12

PROPHETS WHO LIVE BY A MORE SURE WORD

Prophetic relationships are complex, to say the least. What holds you when all is down? What holds you to a real, true friend when people are coming against your friend or even you?

Think about what holds you to God when your ministry seems to be in the toilet because of all the warfare. So what holds you? Consider a more sure word. The concept is absolutely what will always hold you. The prophet must have a more sure word.

When you consider all the people you will meet in your life, consider the confident, successful person who has been through a buffet of storms in their life and stands before you as a testimony. Consider them, but also consider if that could be you.

There is an assurance that showers a prophet of God with favor when we know and understand that God is sovereign and more intelligent than we will ever be. We look at the things we are dealing with and what we go through, and we know that we have something the world can't give us. This is past relationship 101, which is the proving stage.

Looking at Peter's life, we see his witness to the fact that he has been where few have ever been in God. He has something, and that is a deposited experience. He has a more sure word. We all need this.

In *2 Peter 1:19,* Peter speaks of time and experiences, using the term "a more sure word." While this may mean something to Peter, it may not mean as much to us until we are able to examine what we are dealing with.

The daily drama of life speaks to us profoundly. Often, we miss the opportunity to grow and develop because we lack understanding at the moment. There is no price that a prophet can put on having a more sure word in the midst of life's struggle. This is knowing that you will come out of it.

Peter is a classic example for a prophet to study and admire in our efforts to understand that God is still able despite the obstacles we see. We know he is able, because we have a more sure word within.

Having a more sure word of prophecy in your life means understanding God's word and purpose for your life as bigger, larger, and more important than anything else you will ever encounter.

God wants the prophet to understand that they are guided by the author and finisher of their faith. We are guided by God, who is the Alpha and Omega. This is who our God is. He is exactly who he says he is. The key to understanding this type of guidance is to have a more sure word in your life than what you encounter. This means a relationship.

This concept rests in the mature prophet, who has dealt with the indignities of life. Prophet, if God orders your steps, then you will have no problem understanding that everything you go through is a reflection of a more sure word in your life. You are His example to His people. Here is where you must know that all things work together for those who love God.

Prophet, speak to yourself. God has guided me to build me. He has ordained my trials and tribulations. Rather than always blaming satan for my downfalls or shortcomings, have you ever considered that it was the Guider who steered us through trouble and into the path of righteousness for his name's sake?

We quote scriptures and yet we don't have a real deposited experience of them, which means we don't have a more sure word! *Psalms 37:23* says the steps of a good man are ordered by the Lord. Does that mean going through the bad times also?

Does that hold true for pandemics also? Does it hold true for losing family and friends to sickness? How many prophets today know and understand that our steps through this season have been ordered?

Those prophets who have been ordered can have an appreciation for where and what God has and is doing in their lives. When we look at all of our bad times, broken relationships, public ridicule, and struggle to develop and understand and even now, those who God will use are the ones who have a more sure word within them.

Prophets, despite our struggles in life, we must know that God knows, and He will not allow us to just go through something for no reason at all. *Romans 8:28* clearly tells us that all things work together for the good of those who love God. How much do we really love when our bodies are hurting?

How much do we love God when the doctor says he has done all he can do? The reality is that some of our prophetic peers do not have a divine revelation of a more sure word within them.

There is a young man in *Genesis 37,* who was one of the greatest seers of all time. His name is Joseph. We see Joseph go through all types of ups and downs in his life. He was beaten by his brothers and left for dead. He is reported as dead and then sold like a piece of meat into slavery.

God has still ordered his steps. Look at *Genesis 39:2.* In everything he does, the favor of God is with him, as Potiphar observes him. There is something to be said when God has His hand on your life, prophet, and you know that.

Despite what was happening, even a man outside of Christianity could see favor upon Joseph's life. I wonder how many of us have that type of favor upon our lives, and do not realize it.

You're in the midst of the greatest storm of your life, and people are watching. They see assurance, faith, a more sure word in your life. They wonder why and they are in awe of the example you set as they see your good works and seek after your Father who art in heaven. The reality is you are in the middle of the storm.

Joseph's life is a great teacher to us as prophets. He is a seer with an extraordinary gift, and yet he is still lied to and put in jail. We should see that it does not matter how anointed you may be or how you feel; you will suffer for the very sake of the anointing. Unless you really understand you have a more sure word, you will perish.

Joseph is locked in jail and spends two extra years in his situation. Do you think he ever pondered why he is there and for how much longer?

Have you ever thought, "My ministry should be doing this or that? What if this does not happen? Are you saying we should be doing this, or should we be doing that?" Joseph must've had similar thoughts but he held on.

He was human, just like us. The fact is that we see something illustrated in his life in the worst of times should be a great encouragement to us. Knowing that whatever you go through, there is an assurance within you that nothing can shake.

In *Genesis 50:20*, we see Joseph after he has reconciled with his brothers. He says that what was meant for bad, God has turned it around for the good. This should continue to be a classic for every seer to understand.

Those who want to be used by God, those who want what God has for them, and those who say they love God need to embrace Joseph's mentality. Joseph has been done wrong and he is dealing with how to rise above the drama of his own life. This is in the midst of those who have done him dirty.

We strive to move forward, but do we really? Have you ever heard a prophetic peer repeatedly detail how they were done wrong? Maybe you have heard that story for the last 7- 9 years or the total time you have known that seer. You have heard the story so much you memorized it.

Maybe you are that prophet and now you even find yourself in that situation and it just seemed to stay with you. Trouble has become your ministry.

Joseph gives us a key. He finds God in the situation. This is what we all need to do. We must be able to find God in the worst of our storms. God is speaking, directing, and guiding us.

Joseph communicates a great message of growth to his brothers on that day. He tells them that what has happened is past and despite the intent, because of who God is to him. The intent was for the Glory of God. He knows he is the vessel that God has used to place his plan in position for such a time.

Joseph can't help but thank his brothers, who God used to guide him into the position he is currently in. Joseph has been guided to be in the position he finds himself in. He is second in command, and he becomes the greatest administrator the world has ever known. You don't just walk into that type of status; you have to be guided there by a more sure word.

You have to know it also prophet. You have to be able to deal with the situation you find yourself in like Joseph or even Job. Prophet, become sold out and know you are positioned because you have a more sure word.

Say to yourself that you must understand that God is guiding me beside the still waters of life and the raging sea of turmoil. When you think about your life, you have to know that you were blessed even when you did not feel blessed. God will lead His prophets through places that are so dark, and within the darkness. He is there!

You're a prophet called to the nation, and before you were formed in the belly, God knew you, even in the darkness you never imagined. The thing you do not want to do is build a relationship in disobedience because it will cost you greatly. Just because you are a prophet does not mean we will have a relationship. I may respect who you are, but we may never have a relationship unless God wants us to have one. The story of the old prophet of Bethel explains a lot.

CHAPTER 13

THE OLD PROPHET OF BETHEL AND THE OLD PROPHET OF TODAY

The year 931 BC was a long time ago. We see Israel as the central region of wealth, power, and glory. Then suddenly we see the death of King Solomon. Solomon's death has sparked economic and political factors that led to the collapse of the unified kingdom. We now see Israel split into two separate kingdoms.

Let's set order now as Rehoboam, Solomon's son, is the king of the southern kingdom. The southern region is better known as Judah and included Jerusalem and God's temple.

Jeroboam has now ascended to be the first king of the northern kingdom of Israel. King Jeroboam developed his own system of worship. He had not one but two idolatrous shrines with golden calf images *(1 Kings 12)!*

The shrines were strategically placed. One shrine was in the far north of the kingdom, and the other was in Bethel. Bethel is on the border with the southern kingdom of Judah.

This was done on purpose as people in the northern kingdom, traveling south would be tempted to stop off at Bethel and try out the new form of "worship." All this before they could get to Jerusalem.

There is much evil going on and we see, Jeroboam in the middle of intimidating his own people, with his own gods. He even declares his own religious feast day (*1 Kings 14:16 and 15:30*). Jeroboam was known as the "the king who caused Israel to sin."

The history lesson is over now and here is where I need to start prophet. King Jeroboam's sinful religious system does not have God's favor upon it.

God sends a young prophet from Judah to Bethel with a specific assignment to pronounce judgment on the idolatrous form of worship. The divine timing of his arrival is significant, as it underscores the importance of his mission.

The king was offering incense on the false altar of the shrine of the golden calf at this time, as the prophet arrived.

The prophet sees the issue and now prophesies that a future king, who would be a descendant of David named Josiah, would burn the bones of Jeroboam's false priests upon this idolatrous altar.

2 Kings 23:15-16 describes the divine validation of the young prophet's words. As King Jeroboam was put on notice, the altar of the false god split, reinforcing the authority of the young prophet's message and the power of God's intervention.

Here now is where we need to see the actions of the prophet, and the lessons of how to handle yourself are precious. We can look at

Jeroboam, the king as being humbled as God restores his hand from being paralyzed.

We see the King Jeroboam now invites the prophet to come home with him to relax before returning to Judah. The prophet demonstrates an important point as he was offered a reward but did not accept it.

Why? Because God had specifically directed His prophet not to delay or depart from his mission in any way, but to return home directly. The directive was clear. Now, even more issues come upon the prophet.

There is an older prophet who lived in the local area. The gossip of the day has reached his ears, and now he seeks the prophet from Judah.

The balance of listening to God and building relationships now becomes clear. Here we see a prophetic peer and how the relationship manifests here is critical to both the young and old prophet.

The old prophet invites the young prophet to come home with him for some food and fellowship. The young prophet makes a choice and it holds serious issues for his life and the old prophet's life.

In the previous chapter, we discussed that you can be gifted and still totally miss what God has for you, prophet. The mere fact that as your profile grows in the prophetic, your challenges will be greater to discern standards and uphold those standards at the same time.

Here is an opportunity for the young prophet, but is it godly? Realize that some people will have an opportunity to be the undercurrent of your destruction. Simply because you are a prophet of relevance underscores the crucial need for discernment in the prophetic walk of a prophet. Relationships must have a foundation; can you consider what type of relationships you have in your life?

The young prophet because of how he handled the situation for God, now finds himself in a profile he has not been accustomed to. He is now being sought by an older more established prophet. The fellowship needed to build a relationship is being established.

On the outside this looks great, but this is not what God wants for his life. Understand that this is not about the age of the older prophet, but this is about the spirit.

God's specific directions for his assignment were for him to return and not be charmed to do anything else. We now see the older prophet insisted and guess what? The younger prophet was persuaded to turn back and fellowship with him.

The older prophet did something we all know so well as he claimed that the Lord Himself had directed him to bring the younger prophet home, but the older prophet was lying through his teeth.

I will reserve comment here, but how many times have we heard God said this and God said that, as a prophet seeks to get his or her way? Bottom line, the old prophet lied. No disrespect meant.

During dinner, something happens. The word of the Lord really does come to the older prophet. Can you imagine him now denouncing the disobedience of the younger prophet?

Can you imagine this: the young prophet leaves and as he travels, he is killed by a lion, on his way home to Judah! There was another man in the area, but he was not bothered.

The lion now stood guard over the body of the young prophet, which was as a sign to everyone that this was not a freak accident. I cannot help but wonder how the older prophet felt when he heard the news.

Scripture says he retrieved the body of the young prophet and mourned him. He was given an honorable burial.

The old prophet now confirms the word of the younger prophet and asks his sons to bury his own body when he dies next to the prophet from Judah. Prophet, there are three unmistakable lessons to learn here.

1. This lesson is for weak faith and unbelieving prophets.

When God gives you a chance to change your ways and get into a proper relationship with Him. Do it! In *1 Kings 11:38,* Jeroboam before he became king was given a golden opportunity from God. He was given a chance to have a relationship with God, and he did not want it.

Jeroboam ignored the prophet Ahijah's message from God. The consequences of such disobedience are severe and should instill a deep respect for God's directives.

How many times today do we really have the opportunity to have relationships and live in harmony with our brothers and sisters but fail? Like the prophet, we often fail for the wrong reasons.

Yet again, Jeroboam misses the opportunity. The young prophet from Judah has come to confront him; Jeroboam could have repented. The mission was timed precisely so that King Jeroboam would hear the word of God directly from the prophet.

Let's ask the question? Prophet, what about you? Maybe you're gifted but a skeptic, or you simply don't believe that there's a really a prophetic order in God to whom we all must answer.

There are so many prophets that this will affect, and the reality is we must get our relationships and lives in order. Please don't be a prophet like Jeroboam! You simply have created a god that fits only your image! Then again, are you a prophet who always has a better way. We have enough of that today.

Today, far too many prophets have "cut and pasted" the Bible in order to create their own prophetic reality. Take the opportunity to repent and grow right.

2. Lesson for Older Seasoned Prophets

As we have just discussed the two prophets, most likely, the older prophet was a believer in the true God and was not directly a part of Jeroboam's false system of worship.

What else seems to be obvious is that the older prophet did not stir up trouble for himself by speaking out publicly against King Jeroboam.

The indication of him doing what others did was to move south to Judah as others had done, but he remained in Bethel. His status as a local retired prophet with prestige was his claim to fame.

He was stirred up by the actions of the young prophet. We have to consider that he may have been upset that God had left him on the sidelines. Could his passive lifestyle and lack of commitment have made him unsuitable for God's use as a messenger?

Like many prophets, he may have had an exaggerated notion of his own importance as a prophet. There was no good reason for him to lie to the younger prophet. His influence was key to misleading and misdirecting the young prophet.

Mature seasoned prophets have a responsibility to encourage younger prophets to follow the will of the Lord for their lives. But sometimes, improper words of guidance from older prophets can mislead or even manipulate younger prophets. Understand that this is not in age but in the spirit. Age is not the factor most would assume it is.

This is a very serious sin because it may cause younger prophets to miss the Lord's calling for their lives! Sometimes, the problem may be that the older prophet is sincerely mistaken in their counsel. Sometimes, the improper advice is rooted in jealousy.

Sometimes its source is disappointment or bitterness that the Lord has asked a younger prophet to get a job done, and has passed over the older prophet, because the older prophet may have become spiritually unsuited for the job.

Sometimes, older prophets will hinder the leading of the Lord and the proper zeal in the younger prophetic generation because they fear a loss of their own prestige power, or influence.

Mature prophets must understand that they are always under the microscope. You must be careful that you don't hinder or interfere with the Lord's direction in a younger prophet's life and calling.

The older, more mature prophet should sincerely seek the guidance of the Holy Spirit whenever a younger prophet asks you for advice. Do not be too quick to give tainted unscriptural counsel in matters that may affect a younger prophet for a lifetime. This is really serious business of the highest prophetic order.

Before the Lord, examine the honesty of your motives, prophets. Be sure your words of advice are biblical and appropriate. Remember, the life of service of a younger prophet may depend on your mature, wise, and biblical counsel!

There is a lesson for young prophets also. This is a hard lesson because the lesson is hard to see because properly discerning the will of God takes real spiritual sensitivity.

Younger prophets must, first and foremost, learn to follow the will of the Lord (not the will of themselves or their buddies) for their lives! Guidance from the Lord comes in several ways, including the counsel of older prophets.

If you are a young prophet, ask questions to avoid manipulation! The best advice for any prophet is to evaluate what you believe the Lord is directing you to do, then let the Lord confirm His will in a number of different ways, including the council of senior prophetic leadership!

Make sure that senior prophetic leadership is living Christ-honoring lifestyles and has a good knowledge of the Word of God.

Young prophets, stop trying to sell yourself to other prophets. Be yourself. The "I just want to do what the Lord wants me to do, or I just want to do the will of the Lord, "is a worn-out cliche for acceptance that means nothing unless you are willing to live out the word in your mouth to the fullest with your life.

In other words, your boast will not settle your validation of a Christ like relationship, prophet. Only by living it will validate you. This is a lesson the young prophet found out the hard way.

The tale of two prophets is not an easy Bible story to understand. On the surface, it send mixed signals, especially from the old prophet. This was the effort of the enemy to undermine the Word of God by involving the prophet in an ungodly wrong association. How many times do we see this today?

How do you, prophet, act in the presence of strong and subtle temptation? Sometimes, peer communication will invalidate and contradict God and prophetic leadership. Let's be real here.

Prophets often allow themselves to be drawn into a wrong association by disobedience because someone is in an assumed position of relevance like the old prophet.

Let's not forget the jealousy in the prophetic and look as how the old prophet was ready to go to great lengths to discredit the young prophet.

This is one of satan's greatest weapons in the battle against today's contemporary prophet. We see our prophetic peers fall daily because of who they associate with.

Prophets, great honor had been put upon each of us in being used as a witness against evil. God had plainly warned us against being entangled in false associations or people who always stir up drama or trouble.

In spite of God's word, prophetic leadership and just plain common sense, we still see prophets drawn into webs of deceit and drama.

Heb.12:13 encourages us as believers and prophets to test what we know to be lame in our way to see if it will be healed.

Many prophets may firmly reject the first device of evil, only to fall by the second. Prophets, when you see clearly that your association with a group, church or relationship is condemned by the Word of God, take the proper steps so that you stay in the will of God.

The fact that many prophets have left associations condemned by the Word of God, is a testimony against them. They may not have wanted to give, pray, or subject themselves to things that they feel are beneath them.

To go back and align against our own testimony, in principle, is to build against the things we have been on assignment to destroy.

To trust implicitly what you may want to hear, even when we find that there is a contradiction between what the Lord has clearly revealed in His Word and what someone says.

As prophets, we are to obey the Lord Jesus, not men who contradict what God has clearly spoken. We might end up like the young prophet: slain by a lion on the side of the road because of his fellowshipping with the old prophet who was, in reality, a liar who was contradicting the Word of God.

Prophets, you must know the Word of God, because If a prophet or preacher preaches to you a message that is contrary to the clear teaching of scripture, he is a liar and the truth is not in him. Prophet, are you so scared that you won't build the right relationship, that you get along with no one?

As prophets, we must be obedient to God. Many will tell you that, as we reject offers of bread, water, and fellowship that is not a reason for us to not foster good prophetic peer relationships.

There is a reality I now want to explore for us all as you read now about: why don't today's prophets get along or build strong peer and personal relationships?

CHAPTER 14

WHY DON'T TODAY'S PROPHETS GET ALONG OR BUILD RELATIONSHIPS?

Have you ever paused to reflect on your relationships with your fellow prophets today? Have you considered your relationship with God and, importantly, with yourself? Are there any conflicts in your life that need your attention?

Throughout scripture, we find numerous instances of conflicts between prophets. Who would have thought that? I'm urging us to delve deeper into our own relational dynamics.

Heed my warnings throughout this book. God sends people into your life for a reason or a season. Prophets face complex relationships and challenges in fulfilling their divine assignments.

Let's start with Moses and his older brother Aaron, two of the most significant prophets in the Old Testament. Tension would be a soft word to describe the relationship between these two.

In *Exodus 32*, as Moses is on Mount Sinai talking to God, we see that Aaron yields to the people's demands and helps them create a golden calf, which was to be their God.

When Moses returned, conflict was inevitable between the two brothers. Witnessing this difference of opinions and perspectives would have been a profound learning experience.

It's a reminder that observation is a powerful prophetic teacher, offering us insights and perspectives we might not have considered. Never underestimate the power of observation, whether positive or negative.

1 Kings 22:5-28 is the story of Micaiah and Zedekiah. We see that King Ahab consulted 400 prophets. They all predicted success in battle, except for Micaiah, who stood alone in prophesying defeat.

His prophesying resulted in a physical confrontation where Zedekiah struck Micaiah. Wow, the prophets were fighting because of a difference of opinion. Do we see this today? Well, it depends on where you go.

In *Jeremiah 28:1- 17,* look at Jeremiah and Hananiah as they prophesy about the duration of Babylonian captivity. Their differences were public. Hananiah spoke of a quick return, while Jeremiah spoke of a longer time. What ended their conflict was Jeremiah prophesying Hananiah's death, which came to pass.

Conflict within the prophetic is real and a tool of God to mature His prophet. I would like to consider God's will and Jonah's stubbornness. This is not a direct conflict with a prophet but one with God and His will. Here, we see the internal resistance of a prophet to obey God.

Remember when Jonah prophesied to Nineveh in *Jonah 1-4*? Do you remember what God brought him through before he prophesied? A relationship with yourself and a relationship with God is important. Where do you stand on this issue prophet, will it affect your ministry? You must understand what prophetic relationships are and why.

Prophetic relationships are relationships with an abundance of conflicts. Why? Differences in the understanding of God's will, personal pride, different prophetic lineages, and the list can grow even more. Today, we see this over and over as we silently fall out with people and walk around for years with unresolved conflict.

Who wants to admit this? Who wants to be responsible for this behavior? Who, in their right mind, would accept this and know they have a responsibility to live and be a prophet of relevance to God's people?

Today, it is easy to see that relationships between prophets often reveal tension and conflict in our circles. This is especially true as prophets develop. We are all rooted in our unique roles, personalities, and divine assignments.

Please take a long look at this and see that not a whole lot has changed. So many of our relationships are either in the toilet or we struggle to maintain them. The influx of emerging prophets versus mature prophets produces such an environment.

Go back and reread the old prophet and the young prophet. Understand the concept of the previous chapter. We all can and need to work on us before we work on others.

Does your prophetic circle struggle to produce a prophetic hedge, spiritual protection, and guidance that is crucial in prophetic ministry, and thus, the work needed is not done?

So often, we skip it to move to more favorable issues like emotional excitement. We mask our shortcomings with smiles and false humility and do no work. We must do the work that God puts before us.

The mere fact that our teachings, utterances, and mode of operation are different and do not follow the status quo. This does not mean we are wrong; however, it points to the differences we can embrace and learn from.

Have we considered this in our pursuit of relationships? Are we so busy looking for a divine hookup, a term used to describe a perceived divine connection or partnership, that we miss the very essence of relationship building in the prophetic? My answer to this is yes, but you answer for yourself.

Today's prophet is offended at the wink of an eyebrow. It takes so little to offend today's prophets, and the reality is that sometimes the reason is legit, and still, we must push through to accomplish God's plan.

Undoubtedly, our relationships as prophets will reveal and expose our highlighted human limitations and the challenges of conveying God's will. Look and consider this. As a prophet, you must accept that your assignment from God is yours.

I say that because you have been chosen and handpicked by God, and because of that, you have a God-given specific assignment. You can't forget this.

Here, you are to deliver or perform a specific assignment. Your work is often done under the most difficult of circumstances. *Jeremiah 1:4-5* and *Isaiah 6:8* support my point.

These Biblical conflicts reflected the deeper themes of human pride and misunderstanding of God's plan. This is alive and well today in our era.

Despite their differences, the prophets' ultimate purpose was unified: to call people back to God's righteousness. Despite the conflicts, we must do the work of God and trust that He will reveal His master plan.

My goal with this book has been to help us become the best versions of ourselves so we can be the best prophets of God to His people. This is why because we have the gift. We must respect and honor the gift.

This is the reality that the gift belongs to God, and we all have issues that we must attend to. Let us understand that we can fool ourselves because of the notoriety and acclaim that is afforded to the prophetic gift.

Our gift sometimes brings us things we are not ready for. Although we may feel differently, prophet, can you handle this report?

As we journey forth in the prophetic calling, my challenge to you is to cultivate the right type of relationships:
- Relationships that you can disagree with and still be in covenant.
- Relationships that produce honor.

- Relationships are built on respect, dignity, and character, and they build a Godly prophetic community by doing so.

When we honor the prophetic gift, we must also uphold the value and dignity of everyone involved. This, my prophetic friend, is the essence of prophetic relationships. I do have one question for you. Do you have an attitude of responsibility prophet?

CHAPTER 15

THE PROPHET'S ATTITUDE OF RESPONSIBILITY

The prophet's attitude of responsibility is critical. This is a needed attitude to reflect success in the life of the now-generation prophet. The prophet takes total ownership of their actions, decisions, and consequences. They do not blame others. The prophet trusts God.

The prophet's attitude of responsibility is a process within the prophetic development of that prophet. The involvement of embracing accountability, reliability, and proactiveness is all active. The character within the prophet is built through these actions. Character is essential to addressing challenges while maintaining integrity and self-discipline.

The prophet's attitude of responsibility and prophetic peer relationships are interconnected.

The prophet must know that the attitude of responsibility involves personal accountability, self-regulation, and ownership of actions and decisions. This takes on a new meaning with the prophet's prophetic peer and personal relationships.

The prophet's peer and personal relationships are based on mutual trust, companionship and shared values. Can you see why I will reflect again on the old prophet and the young prophet in chapter 13?

We can clearly see that peer influence can shape attitudes and behaviors and can produce risky actions. The young prophet was no different from a young prophet today, seeking validation from an older, more established prophet. We all want to be accepted and esteemed, but that is not the plan of God. Let us never forget we are the agents of change.

As prophets, our individual behavior and ethical decision-making are key to fulfilling our commitments. As responsible prophets, we need to seek to enhance our relationships with peers and personal acquaintances. We do this as we discern our peers and friends of like mind.

Cooperation among our prophetic peers is critical. It is essential as we seek to understand the power of positive prophetic peer relationships.

The reality of positive prophetic peer relationships can reinforce a prophet's responsible attitude, even when the prophet's personal relationships seek to affect that prophet.

Our prophetic peer relationships are so important in our lives. This is because so many prophets suffer through what they go through in their personal lives.

Finally, they reach a point where being unknown is no longer an option, and the need for real peer support is vital as the prophet grows in their calling.

The prophet's attitude of responsibility is tied to the prophet's personal growth. We will deal with self-reflection, resilience, and mindfulness as we respond constructively to situations beyond our control. We learn how to depend on God with this type of attitude.

The prophet's attitude of responsibility is a responsible way the prophet builds trust with prophetic peers and others. How can a prophet develop a more responsible attitude in daily life? Consider these practical steps:

1. Take ownership of your life and actions: Prophet, you must acknowledge your actions and decisions and avoid blaming others for outcomes.
2. Set personal prophetic goals in your life: Prophet, it is your responsibility to define clear, actionable objectives for your personal motivation and focus.
3. Understand the challenge: Prophet, you must view obstacles as unique personal opportunities for growth rather than setbacks.
4. Always, yes, always ensure you practice gratitude: Make notes, prophet, and keep a gratitude journal to foster positivity and accountability in your life. No one has to see it but you.
5. Ensure you always surround yourself with positivity, even amid a personal storm: Spend time with prophets and prophetic people who inspire responsibility and optimism. Develop a daily routine of structured habits that will reinforce your discipline and reliability.

Growth is a process that happens in its own way for each of us. The great opportunity we all have is to participate in the process. How we participate in the process is up to us. Moses was different from Abraham. Abraham was different from Jeremiah, and he was different from Joseph.

Ladies none of you were exactly like Deborah or Hulda or the wife of Isaiah. We are all different. I relate to the Prophet Samuel, but my journey in growth has not been like his.

Each of us must have an attitude of responsibility. As we look at our lives, we can see that our prophetic relationships have great value. Do not underestimate prophetic relationships, as they will reflect on our relationship with God.

Finally, realize that when God wants to make a prophet powerful, He strips that prophet and tears up many of that prophet's relationships. The prophet who walks with God will often walk alone because God desires that prophet to sacrifice.

Remember that the next time you find yourself in a group and you seem all alone. Prophet get your relationship with God in place so your prophetic relationships will prosper. I pray *Psalms 91* over your life.

ABOUT THE AUTHOR

Apostle Ken Cox started serving God in 1994 after a series of unforeseen life failures. Out of the military and seemly starting life over again, by 2000, Apostle Cox had found his life calling as a Prophet. The challenge of learning and understanding presented a new frontier. Apostle Cox dove into the process and has now emerged as a well-traveled prophet who serves the Body of Christ as an Apostle.

Apostle Cox, along with his wife, Prophetess Sabina Cox are the leaders of Where Eagles Fly Fellowship Inc., a fellowship of prophets and apostle across the USA and beyond who are dedicated and focused on establishing the prophetic gift back into society as they raise up prophets around the country and abroad.

Apostle Cox and Prophetess Cox are available for Revivals, Conferences and Meetings. They have been featured in meetings and sought-after to teach and instruct the prophetic for ministries seeking to learn more about the gift. Apostle and Prophetess Cox have 3 children and 6 grandkids as of this writing and currently reside in Durham, NC. Contact them through the Where Eagles Fly office at 919-695-3375 or 919-213-1328 or at www.whereeaglesfly.us.

He is also the author of the following books:

The Prophet In The Wilderness

Luciferian Spirit Among The Prophets
Meeting The Prophet In My Reflection
Prophet Called to a Cross Culture
Visualization, The Prophet Sees In Adullam
The Prophetic Staff
The Mentality of the Prophetic Staff
The Soul of The Prophet's Health
The Unseen War of the Issachar Seer's Soul
The Soul of the Issachar Seer
A Prophet In The Moment: Understanding Where You Are At In The Prophetic Process
The Prophetic Arc

INDEX

5

5-fold ministry, 55

A

Aaron, 76, 121, 122
Abraham, 38, 129
accountability, 127, 129
adult, 56, 57, 60
adultery, 9
Alpha, 104
altar, 78, 111
anger, 23, 24, 31, 51, 76, 83
animal, 52
anointed, 5, 8, 9, 19, 39, 49, 56, 72, 106
anointing, 53, 72, 106
Apostle, 12, 60, 62, 131
Ark, 40
armor bearer, 13
assignments, 18, 57, 86, 87, 94, 121, 123
atmosphere, 13, 20, 22, 27, 28

attitude, 21, 49, 64, 73, 75, 76, 126, 127, 128, 129, 130
authority, 43, 59, 65, 70, 71, 72, 78, 111

B

Babylon, 64
bank account, 93
Barak, 68
battle, 40, 50, 52, 63, 68, 118, 122
behavior, 57, 59, 71, 74, 75, 76, 78, 123, 128
beliefs, 15
believers, 55, 119
Bethel, 17, 73, 109, 110, 111, 115
Bible, 3, 36, 39, 41, 72, 73, 115, 118
biblical counsel, 117
bitter, 14, 65
blame, 7, 8, 24, 30, 53, 57, 63, 127
blessing, 10, 21, 25, 27, 31, 38, 43, 75
blessings, 38, 39, 46, 94
bones, 67, 88, 111
book, 1, 2, 3, 78, 121, 125
boss, 7, 63, 75
bosses, 98
boy, 5
brothers, 17, 48, 49, 106, 107, 108, 114, 122
business, 5, 6, 66, 72, 73, 93, 117

C

celebration, 45
ceremony, 72
challenges, 15, 112, 121, 124, 127
chaos, 4, 23, 30, 97, 99

child, 4, 5, 6, 7, 8, 9, 27, 48, 56, 57, 58, 59, 60
childish, 56, 57, 58, 59, 60
children, 21, 23, 28, 29, 30, 48, 52, 57, 58, 59, 60, 63, 80, 99, 100, 131
Christ, 20, 24, 27, 31, 40, 41, 42, 44, 56, 58, 59, 74, 75, 93, 117, 118, 131
Christians, 74, 78, 79
church, 24, 31, 55, 80, 81, 92, 119
churches, 44, 70, 73
clothing, 45
coach, 78
communion, 79
compliance, 76
conferences, 92
conflict, 7, 9, 10, 40, 49, 50, 51, 53, 54, 83, 86, 122, 123
consequences, 4, 7, 15, 83, 114, 127
conversation, 81, 82, 83, 84, 85, 86, 87
conviction, 15, 17
cornerstone, 55
courage, 15, 17, 57
covenant, 2, 13, 43, 88, 98, 125
crime, 74
cultures, 13, 82
curse, 36, 37, 42, 45, 73
customers, 75

D

daughters, 11, 13
David, 3, 4, 5, 6, 7, 8, 9, 10, 11, 48, 49, 50, 51, 52, 58, 59, 111
dead, 4, 5, 8, 66, 84, 106
death, 9, 14, 15, 60, 66, 87, 110, 122
Deborah, 68, 130
deception, 41, 42

decision-maker, 24
dedication, 15, 100
deliverance, 91, 93, 96
demonic strongholds, 93
demons, 46
desire, 2, 9, 37, 50
destiny, 36, 54, 55, 56, 57, 58, 60, 92
destruction, 112
determination, 15
development, 13, 14, 21, 22, 27, 28, 29, 33, 57, 85, 102, 127
devil, 7, 9, 35
dilemma, 21, 27
dinner, 113
disappointment, 116
discernment, 8, 14, 54, 70, 71, 112
discipline, 8, 36, 38, 45, 85, 97, 127, 129
discomfort, 6
discouragement, 89
disobedience, 37, 45, 88, 109, 113, 114, 118
disrespect, 10, 23, 29, 69, 71, 72, 73, 74, 75, 76, 77, 78, 80, 113
doctor, 106
doubt, 5, 89, 98, 100, 101
drama, 4, 7, 8, 9, 23, 30, 104, 107, 118
dry land, 89, 90, 91, 93, 95

E

ear, 38
earth, 78, 81, 88
educate, 75
Egypt, 21, 28, 40, 99
Egyptian, 86
elders, 4

elephant, 41, 42
elevation, 51, 53
Eliab, 49
Elijah, 12, 16, 17, 90
Elisha, 12, 16, 17, 73, 74, 76, 90
emotions, 31, 37, 49, 51, 52, 53, 54, 86
employment, 93, 98
empowerment, 19, 20, 42
Encourage, 54
enemy, 39, 93, 94, 95, 118
Ephesians, 40, 55
equation, 6, 25, 32, 44
Evil, 63
Ezekiel, 63, 64, 65, 66, 67, 81, 83, 84, 85, 88, 93

F

faith, 15, 16, 22, 23, 25, 28, 29, 30, 31, 44, 50, 69, 70, 86, 87, 89, 90, 91, 93, 94, 101, 104, 106, 114
family, 24, 31, 41, 49, 52, 76, 80, 98, 100, 105
fasting, 46, 92
father, 13, 16, 48, 78
favor, 103, 106, 111
fear, 24, 31, 40, 44, 83, 86, 116
feelings, 1, 10, 51, 54, 64, 83, 90
fellowship, 55, 89, 90, 112, 113, 120, 131
finances, 44, 46, 93, 94
fish, 63
floodgates, 46
food, 4, 45, 78, 112
fortune, 47
foundation, 55, 59, 80, 95, 102, 113
friend, 1, 2, 47, 51, 53, 103, 126

friends, 2, 13, 49, 53, 75, 76, 94, 98, 105, 128
frustration, 23, 83

G

generation, 2, 6, 8, 17, 36, 61, 69, 75, 77, 88, 91, 116, 127
gifts, 1, 55, 57, 91, 92, 96, 97, 98
Gilgal, 17
goals, 47, 129
God, 2, 3, 4, 5, 6, 7, 8, 9, 10, 13, 15, 17, 18, 19, 20, 21, 22, 23, 24, 25, 26, 27, 28, 29, 30, 31, 32, 33, 34, 35, 36, 37, 38, 39, 40, 42, 43, 44, 45, 46, 48, 49, 50, 51, 53, 54, 56, 57, 58, 60, 61, 62, 63, 64, 65, 66, 67, 68, 70, 71, 72, 73, 74, 75, 76, 77, 78, 79, 80, 81, 82, 83, 84, 85, 86, 87, 88, 89, 90, 91, 92, 93, 94, 95, 96, 97, 98, 99, 100, 101, 102, 103, 104, 105, 106, 107, 108, 109, 110, 111, 112, 113, 114, 115, 117, 118, 119, 120, 121, 122, 123, 124, 125, 127, 128, 129, 130, 131
Goliath, 49, 50
gospel, 1, 59
gossip, 10, 16, 52, 71, 100, 112
guidance, 82, 104, 116, 124

H

Hananiah, 122
hard work, 36, 97, 100
hardship, 90
harvest, 39, 93
heart, 3, 8, 37, 45, 71
heaven, 38, 45, 46, 106
herb, 14
history, 63, 111
holy, 70, 80
Holy Spirit, 43, 63, 72, 116

honor, 8, 12, 16, 25, 32, 60, 72, 78, 81, 87, 118, 125, 126
hope, 64, 67, 88
hopelessness, 64
household, 37
housing, 45
human, 14, 73, 85, 107, 124, 125
humanity, 1, 42
humility, 7, 16, 25, 32, 87, 101, 124
hyssop, 48

I

influence, 1, 57, 58, 59, 77, 116, 128
inspiration, 1, 60
instruments, 90
Intercession, 92
Isaiah, 13, 26, 32, 88, 125, 130
Israel, 9, 13, 17, 21, 23, 28, 29, 30, 39, 49, 68, 72, 84, 100, 110, 111

J

jealous, 12
Jeremiah, 13, 68, 122, 125, 129
Jericho, 16, 17
Jeroboam, 110, 111, 112, 114, 115
Jerusalem, 110, 111
Jesse, 48, 49
Jesus, 41, 55, 68, 90, 119
Jews, 63, 64, 66, 67, 78, 80
Job, 38, 54, 63, 108
Jonah, 122, 123
Joseph, 90, 106, 107, 108, 129
journey, 1, 2, 15, 22, 58, 86, 125, 130

Judah, 110, 111, 112, 113, 114, 115
judgment, 9, 74, 111

K

key, 1, 13, 15, 25, 26, 32, 33, 51, 57, 75, 83, 93, 94, 95, 102, 104, 108, 116, 128
kids, 57, 73
king, 3, 48, 49, 58, 65, 110, 111, 112, 114
kingdom, 46, 75, 79, 110, 111
Kingdom, 44, 45, 95
knowledge, 4, 5, 37, 57, 117
Knowledge, 37

L

language, 65, 71
laws, 43, 88
leader, 9, 16, 23, 24, 29, 30, 31, 37, 49, 52, 60
leadership, 8, 18, 22, 29, 97, 117, 118
lesson, 5, 6, 8, 16, 24, 27, 30, 31, 34, 62, 66, 86, 111, 114, 117, 118
Levitical priesthood, 72
liar, 119
library, 92
life, 3, 4, 5, 6, 7, 8, 9, 13, 16, 21, 22, 24, 26, 27, 28, 29, 30, 32, 33, 34, 35, 36, 41, 42, 43, 45, 46, 47, 48, 49, 50, 51, 52, 53, 54, 56, 57, 58, 60, 62, 64, 65, 66, 67, 68, 77, 80, 81, 84, 85, 86, 87, 92, 94, 95, 96, 97, 98, 99, 100, 101, 103, 104, 105, 106, 107, 108, 112, 113, 116, 117, 121, 127, 129, 130, 131
livestock, 48
Lord, 5, 40, 41, 43, 45, 63, 67, 74, 78, 79, 88, 89, 90, 91, 105, 113, 116, 117, 119
love, 36, 41, 44, 54, 56, 57, 67, 71, 82, 84, 87, 89, 102, 105, 106, 107

Luciferian Spirit, 132

M

Malachi, 45, 65, 78, 79, 80
manipulation, 117
mannerisms, 4, 38
mantle, 8, 10, 16, 21, 28, 29, 50
Marriage, 63
Mary, 68
meetings, 18, 131
message, 10, 64, 65, 66, 68, 70, 71, 77, 108, 111, 114, 119
metaphor, 58
Micah, 39
Micaiah, 122
microscope, 116
Midianites, 39
ministries, 1, 80, 91, 131
ministry, 24, 31, 41, 55, 57, 92, 93, 94, 95, 103, 107, 108, 123, 124
miracle, 25, 31
Miriam, 76
mirror, 3
misfortune, 37
mission, 66, 84, 100, 111, 112, 114
mockery, 15, 71, 72
money, 36, 37, 38, 41, 42, 44, 93
Moses, 21, 22, 23, 24, 27, 28, 29, 30, 31, 33, 34, 76, 85, 86, 90, 99, 100, 121, 122, 129
motives, 87, 117
murder, 9

N

Nabu, 12
Nathan, 4, 5, 10
nation, 37, 45, 77, 85, 109
Nineveh, 123

O

obedience, 35, 45, 94
offense, 70
offerings, 45
Omega, 104
opinion, 1, 98, 99, 122
opportunity, 22, 29, 40, 49, 50, 87, 90, 99, 104, 112, 114, 115, 129
oppression, 39

P

pain, 8, 38, 65, 67, 84, 85, 90
Palestine, 88
pandemics, 105
parents, 41, 73, 98
pastor, 7
patience, 97
Paul, 60, 62, 77
peers, 16, 18, 19, 49, 51, 60, 70, 76, 93, 97, 98, 101, 106, 118, 128, 129
perceptions, 53, 82
perseverance, 97, 98
persistence, 97
personalities, 13, 15, 77, 123
Peter, 104
Philistines, 51, 52
Potiphar, 106

poverty, 35, 36, 37, 38, 39, 40, 41, 42, 43, 44
power, 1, 15, 37, 39, 59, 60, 65, 67, 86, 92, 110, 111, 116, 122, 128
prayer, 5, 6, 54, 87, 92
prayers, 25, 32, 46
preacher, 41, 119
pride, 86, 87, 123, 125
priests, 72, 78, 79, 80, 111
promises, 36, 38, 43, 44
prophecy, 104
prophet, 1, 2, 3, 4, 6, 7, 8, 9, 13, 14, 15, 17, 18, 19, 20, 21, 22, 23, 24, 25, 26, 27, 28, 29, 30, 31, 32, 33, 35, 36, 37, 40, 42, 43, 46, 48, 49, 50, 51, 52, 53, 54, 55, 56, 57, 58, 60, 61, 63, 64, 65, 66, 67, 68, 69, 70, 71, 72, 73, 74, 75, 76, 77, 78, 79, 80, 82, 83, 84, 85, 86, 87, 89, 90, 91, 92, 93, 94, 95, 96, 97, 98, 99, 100, 101, 102, 103, 104, 106, 108, 109, 111, 112, 113, 114, 115, 116, 117, 118, 119, 122, 123, 124, 125, 126, 127, 128, 129, 130, 131
Prophet Sees In Adullam, 132
prophetic, 1, 2, 3, 4, 5, 10, 12, 13, 14, 15, 16, 17, 18, 21, 22, 23, 24, 25, 27, 28, 29, 31, 33, 38, 49, 50, 53, 54, 57, 58, 59, 70, 71, 74, 75, 76, 86, 92, 93, 94, 95, 96, 97, 99, 101, 102, 106, 107, 112, 115, 116, 117, 118, 120, 122, 123, 124, 125, 126, 127, 128, 129, 130, 131
Prophetic Arc, 132
Prophetic Culture, 18
Prophetic Process, 132
Prophetic Staff, 132
prophets, 2, 3, 5, 6, 7, 8, 9, 10, 12, 13, 14, 15, 16, 17, 18, 19, 20, 21, 22, 23, 24, 25, 26, 27, 28, 29, 30, 31, 32, 33, 35, 36, 39, 40, 41, 42, 43, 44, 45, 46, 50, 55, 56, 57, 58, 59, 60, 61, 63, 64, 65, 66, 68, 69, 70, 71, 72, 73, 74, 75, 76, 77, 78, 85, 88, 89, 90, 92, 94, 95, 96, 97, 98, 105, 106, 108, 114, 115, 116, 117, 118, 119, 120, 121, 122, 123, 124, 125, 128, 129, 131
Prosperity, 35

R

Ramah, 17
recognition, 24, 31, 101, 102
reflections, 6
Rehoboam, 110
relationships, 1, 2, 3, 12, 13, 14, 15, 16, 19, 48, 56, 59, 71, 74, 82, 83, 88, 91, 98, 99, 101, 102, 103, 105, 112, 113, 114, 115, 120, 121, 123, 124, 125, 126, 127, 128, 130
religion, 17
repent, 5, 7, 84, 91, 115
reputation, 52
resources, 39, 44, 45, 94
respect, 10, 16, 22, 23, 29, 72, 76, 77, 78, 79, 80, 81, 82, 85, 92, 109, 114, 125, 126
responsibility, 7, 8, 15, 52, 53, 116, 123, 126, 127, 129, 130
revelation, 60, 106
revivals, 92
riches, 37, 39, 43, 80
righteousness, 46, 79, 95, 105, 125
robbery, 45
roses, 89

S

sadness, 64
saga, 51, 52, 83
salvation, 90
Samuel, 4, 5, 8, 12, 13, 40, 48, 49, 50, 68, 130
Satan, 40, 41, 63
Saul, 49, 50, 51
Savior, 90
scandal, 4, 5, 6

School of the Prophet, 12, 18, 19
schools, 13, 17, 76, 92
seed of access, 16
selfish, 58, 60, 87, 99
self-regulation, 127
servants, 4, 5, 8, 42, 56, 63, 74
shame, 37, 51
sheep, 48, 63
siblings, 98
sick, 4
signature, 16
signs, 97
sin, 45, 48, 89, 92, 111, 116
sisters, 17, 114
slavery, 24, 30, 106
snow, 48
social media, 66, 100
society, 12, 17, 24, 31, 100, 131
Solomon, 43, 110
sons, 10, 11, 13, 16, 17, 48, 63, 68, 114
sorrow, 84, 90
soul, 4, 7, 21, 25, 27, 31, 35
Soul, 3, 4, 132
spectators, 36
Spectrum, 10
spirit realm, 14
spiritual warfare, 46
stewardship, 43, 96, 102
storm, 48, 62, 106, 129
strength, 8, 20, 52, 62, 90
suffering, 6, 65
support system, 99

T

tax, 44
teachers, 41
temptation, 118
testimony, 103, 119
The Gathering of the Wild Gourds, 13
throne, 9, 65
tithes, 45
tongue, 60, 77
torment, 7
training, 23, 30, 45, 74, 90, 92
transportation, 45
trauma, 20, 27
tribulations, 62, 105
troops, 5
trophy, 90
trouble, 5, 6, 61, 62, 63, 64, 65, 66, 67, 68, 69, 105, 115, 118
trumpet, 40
trust, 17, 20, 21, 22, 23, 27, 28, 29, 30, 38, 39, 54, 61, 62, 63, 65, 66, 67, 86, 90, 91, 101, 119, 125, 128, 129
turmoil, 108

U

utterance, 15, 94

V

validation, 39, 51, 56, 111, 118, 128
vehicle, 65
victory, 40
violation, 77

vision, 52, 65, 67, 88, 89
Visualization, 132
voice, 1, 44

W

war, 39, 40, 93
warfare, 93, 94, 95, 103
warriors, 52
weakness, 20, 22
wealth, 38, 39, 42, 43, 44, 93, 94, 110
Where Eagles Fly Fellowship Inc, 131
whisper, 8
wife, 4, 58, 66, 67, 84, 85, 130, 131
wilderness, 24, 27, 30, 33, 45, 85, 86, 100
wisdom, 24, 30, 36, 40, 101
wives, 52
woman, 4, 56, 59, 76
wonders, 97
world, 1, 5, 14, 24, 30, 45, 49, 56, 65, 69, 73, 75, 76, 79, 80, 90, 98, 103, 108
worship, 43, 54, 71, 80, 110, 111, 115

Z

Zedekiah, 122
Ziklag, 52

www.ingramcontent.com/pod-product-compliance
Lightning Source LLC
LaVergne TN
LVHW021827060526
838201LV00058B/3544